~~HATE~~ LOVE SPEECH

A BOOK ABOUT MORALITY
AND HOMOSEXUAL RELATIONSHIPS

DAVID ROBINSON

E/P™
ETHICS PUBLISHING

LOVE SPEECH
by David Robinson

www.lovespeechbook.com

Published by Ethics Publishing, 1004 North Hwy 92,

Jefferson City, Tennessee 37760
info@ethicspublishing.com

(865) 475-8339, Fax: (865) 381-1977

International Standard Book Number:
978-0-9896315-7-0

Printed in the United States of America

Author's Note:

This book is not a research paper. It is a book on ethics. Many of the ideas I explore in this book have been spoken or written by others before. If these were new ideas they would probably not be very helpful. Ethics is a study that has developed over thousands of years. Humans have always tried to discover and understand what is right and wrong. Some of these notions of morality have stood the test of time, and some have not. Many of the ethical ideas that have not performed well under scrutiny in the past seem to consistently reappear in the present in new forms. It is the job of those who care about morality to identify and refute these ideas in whatever disguise they may wear today. I have not attempted to follow these ideas back to their roots. If my failure to do so offends anyone, I apologize in advance.

As you read, I want you to remember the reason I wrote this book. I wrote this book for you. I wrote this book because I love all people. This book is about love. What I have written may cause pain for some, but love sometimes must inflict pain to bring healing. "Faithful are the wounds of a friend; but the kisses of an enemy are deceitful" (Proverbs 27:6). I know there will be some people who will not like what I have written, but please understand that I wrote these words with humility and with an intense love for the intended reader. I ask only that this book be read in that context, with the same level of respect, tolerance, and openness that you would ask of me if you were expressing ideas you thought important. I can only hope that those who do read this book read all of it. You may read portions of this book that make you angry, but, if you finish the book, you will at least realize that my intentions are loving. I do not desire to harm anyone. I do hope that for some, this book will lead to peace, and for many, this book will lead to hope. Please remember, as you read, that I love you.

David Robinson

On a beautiful spring day in Tennessee

The Greatest Commandment

Hearing that Jesus had silenced the
Sadducees, the Pharisees got
together. One of them, an expert in the
law, tested him with this
question: "Teacher, which is the greatest
commandment in the Law?"

Jesus replied: "'Love the Lord your God
with all your heart and with all your
soul and with all your mind.' This is the
first and greatest commandment. And
the second is like it: 'Love your neighbor
as yourself.' All the Law and the
Prophets hang on these two
commandments."

Matthew 22:34-46

*For my all of my brothers and sisters
who struggle with same-sex attractions.
I love You.*

TABLE of CONTENTS

Foreword

Chapters:

LOVE SPEECH

FOREWORD

We cannot begin to analyze issues like the ones we will deal with in this book without understanding that ideas have consequences. Neither can we attempt to tackle any ethical question without understanding, whatever our conclusions may be, real people will be affected. The issue of whether it is morally right or wrong to engage in homosexual sex is now facing our society in a way that cannot be ignored. This issue is immensely divisive. It is immensely important. One of the reasons this question weighs so heavily in my thoughts is because one of my closest friends identifies as a lesbian. We will call my friend Cara. I love Cara and I love everyone else, warts and all. Because of that love, and my desire to write truthfully but gently to those who read this book, I think it is important to state something about someone who will be affected by these words before we get to the heart of the matter. Specifically, I want to state something about my beloved friend Cara. What I write about Cara is honestly and deeply held.

In many ways Cara is advanced. She understands much of the natural moral law, especially as it informs us about how people ought to treat others. Cara has a generosity of more than material charity; a true generosity of spirit that few others I know possess. One would be hard pressed to find any person who Cara has befriended that would not assure you of his belief that Cara would climb mountains for him if the need demanded. This belief would be true because Cara is a true friend. She loves people. She is kind and accepting to those who may not find a friendly face from others. She is quick to forgive and slow to hold a grudge. She gives each person his or her due with encouragement and sincere respect. She would sooner be hurt than demand justice from those who would take advantage of her.

She has her beliefs and opinions and she is not too shy to share them, but she works to live at peace with others. Cara has been through a lot. Cara has been hurt. She has been hurt by me more than I would probably like to believe, and she has been hurt by others more than I can bear to consider. Through it all, she has shown a triumph of courage and class. Cara tries to be real. She is authentic even when dealing with those who are not. She gives the benefit of the doubt, often to her own hurt. Cara loves people.

People also love Cara. She has so captured the hearts of others that I have seen them go to great lengths to help and care for her. I do not only speak of family members who have a natural tie to her through blood or marriage, but of people who were strangers to her before she entered their lives. She has developed many friendships, true friendships. Cara is intelligent. Cara is creative. Cara is talented. Cara is a special human being. God has blessed Cara.

Cara is my friend and I love her…very, very much.

THE EMPERORS NEW CLOTHES

Before we begin please read this story. It is an old story but the truth it suggests is a truth we will see again in the following pages.

MANY, many years ago lived an emperor, who thought so much of new clothes that he spent all his money in order to obtain them; his only ambition was to be always well dressed. He did not care for his soldiers, and the theatre did not amuse him; the only thing, in fact, he thought anything of was to drive out and show a new suit of clothes. He had a coat for every hour of the day; and as one would say of a king "He is in his cabinet," so one could say of him, "The emperor is in his dressing-room."

The great city where he resided was very gay; every day many strangers from all parts of the globe arrived. One day two swindlers came to this city; they made people believe that they were weavers, and declared they could manufacture the finest cloth to be imagined. Their colours and patterns, they said, were not only exceptionally beautiful, but the clothes made of their material possessed the wonderful quality of being invisible to any man who was unfit for his office or unpardonably stupid.

"That must be wonderful cloth," thought the emperor. "If I were to be dressed in a suit made of this cloth I should be able to find out which men in my empire were unfit for their places, and I could distinguish the clever from the stupid. I must have this cloth woven for me without delay." And he gave a large sum of money to the swindlers, in advance, that they should set to work without any loss of time. They set up two looms, and pretended to be very hard at work, but they did nothing whatever on the looms. They asked for the finest silk and the most precious gold-cloth; all they got they did away with, and worked at the empty looms till late at night.

"I should very much like to know how they are getting on with the cloth," thought the emperor. But he felt rather uneasy when he remembered that he who was not fit for his office could not see it. Personally, he was of opinion that he had nothing to fear, yet he thought it advisable to send somebody else first to see how matters stood. Everybody in the town knew what a remarkable quality the stuff possessed, and all were anxious to see how bad or stupid their neighbours were.

"I shall send my honest old minister to the weavers," thought the emperor. "He can judge best how the stuff looks, for he is intelligent, and nobody understands his office better than he."

The good old minister went into the room where the swindlers sat before the empty looms. "Heaven preserve us!" he thought, and opened his eyes wide, "I cannot see anything at all," but he did not say so. Both swindlers requested him to come near, and asked him if he did not admire the exquisite pattern and the beautiful colours, pointing to the empty looms. The poor old minister tried his very best, but he could see nothing, for there was nothing to be seen. "Oh dear," he thought, "can I be so stupid? I should never have thought so, and nobody must know it! Is it possible that I am not fit for my office? No, no, I cannot say that I was unable to see the cloth."

"Now, have you got nothing to say?" said one of the swindlers, while he pretended to be busily weaving.

"Oh, it is very pretty, exceedingly beautiful," replied the old minister looking through his glasses.

"What a beautiful pattern, what brilliant colours! I shall tell the emperor that I like the cloth very much."

"We are pleased to hear that," said the two weavers, and described to him the colours and explained the curious pattern. The old minister listened attentively, that he might relate to the emperor what they said; and so he did.

Now the swindlers asked for more money, silk and gold-cloth, which they required for weaving. They kept everything for themselves, and not a thread came near the loom, but they continued, as hitherto, to work at the empty looms.

Soon afterwards the emperor sent another honest courtier to the weavers to see how they were getting on, and if the cloth was nearly finished. Like the old minister, he looked and looked but could see nothing, as there was nothing to be seen.

"Is it not a beautiful piece of cloth?" asked the two swindlers, showing and explaining the magnificent pattern, which, however, did not exist.

"I am not stupid," said the man. "It is therefore my good appointment for which I am not fit. It is very strange, but I must not let any one know it;" and he praised the cloth, which he did not see, and expressed his joy at the beautiful colours and the fine pattern. "It is very excellent," he said to the emperor.

Everybody in the whole town talked about the precious cloth. At last the emperor wished to see it himself, while it was still on the loom. With a number of courtiers, including the two who had already been there, he went to the two clever swindlers, who now worked as hard as they could, but without using any thread.

"Is it not magnificent?" said the two old statesmen who had been there before. "Your Majesty must admire the colours and the pattern." And then they pointed to the empty looms, for they imagined the others could see the cloth.

"What is this?" thought the emperor, "I do not see anything at all. That is terrible! Am I stupid? Am I unfit to be emperor? That would indeed be the most dreadful thing that could happen to me."

"Really," he said, turning to the weavers, "your cloth has our most gracious approval;" and nodding contentedly he looked at the empty loom, for he did not like to say that he saw nothing. All his attendants, who were with him, looked and looked, and although they could not see anything more than the others, they said, like the emperor, "It is very beautiful." And all advised him to wear the new magnificent clothes at a great procession which was soon to take place. "It is magnificent, beautiful, excellent," one heard them say; everybody seemed to be delighted, and the emperor appointed the two swindlers "Imperial Court weavers."

The whole night previous to the day on which the procession was to take place, the swindlers pretended to work, and burned more than sixteen candles. People should see that they were busy to finish the emperor's new suit. They pretended to take the cloth from the loom, and worked about in the air with big scissors, and sewed with needles without thread, and said at last: "The emperor's new suit is ready now."

The emperor and all his barons then came to the hall; the swindlers held their arms up as if they held something in their hands and said: "These are the trousers!" "This is the coat!" and "Here is the cloak!" and so on. "They are all as light as a cobweb, and one must feel as if one had nothing at all upon the body; but that is just the beauty of them."

"Indeed!" said all the courtiers; but they could not see anything, for there was nothing to be seen.

"Does it please your Majesty now to graciously undress," said the swindlers, "that we may assist your Majesty in putting on the new suit before the large looking-glass?"

The emperor undressed, and the swindlers pretended to put the new suit upon him, one piece after another; and the emperor looked at himself in the glass from every side.

"How well they look! How well they fit!" said all. "What a beautiful pattern! What fine colours! That is a magnificent suit of clothes!"

The master of the ceremonies announced that the bearers of the canopy, which was to be carried in the procession, were ready.

"I am ready," said the emperor. "Does not my suit fit me marvellously?" Then he turned once more to the looking-glass, that people should think he admired his garments.

The chamberlains, who were to carry the train, stretched their hands to the ground as if they lifted up a train, and pretended to hold something in their hands; they did not like people to know that they could not see anything.

The emperor marched in the procession under the beautiful canopy, and all who saw him in the street and out of the windows exclaimed: "Indeed, the emperor's new suit is incomparable! What a long train he has! How well it fits him!" Nobody wished to let others know he saw nothing, for then he would have been unfit for his office or too stupid. Never emperor's clothes were more admired.

"But he has nothing on at all," said a little child at last. "Good heavens! listen to the voice of an innocent child," said the father, and one whispered to the other what the child had said. "But he has nothing on at all," cried at last the whole people. That made a deep impression upon the emperor, for it seemed to him that they were right; but he thought to himself, "Now I must bear up to the end." And the chamberlains walked with still greater dignity, as if they carried the train which did not exist.

THE END

Fairy tales of Andersen by Hans Christian Andersen, translated by H. P. Paull (1872)

CHAPTER 1

<u>What are We Arguing About?</u>

THE PROBLEM

Because I love my friend Cara, I would like nothing more than to be able to celebrate all her achievements and all her joys. Unfortunately, there is a belief that we do not share, a fundamental value that divides us, an issue which Cara and I both believe is very important. This issue is whether or not it is morally right to engage in homosexual sexual relations.

In the following chapters I will set out the reasoning for my understanding of the nature of sexual relationships in general, and homosexual sexual relationships in particular. I want each person who reads this book to see this issue for what it is, in all of its complexity. This issue has boundaries that no one on either side is willing to cross. Make no mistake; taking either side of this issue will cause you to alienate someone, often the person you alienate will be a close friend or family member. This issue is dividing society. It is dividing political parties. It is dividing friendships and it is dividing families.

Is it morally right for two people of the same gender to have sex? This question must be answered by each thoughtful individual, and no talking point or clichéd slogan should persuade you one way or the other. To find the truth, we must work through the evidence. We must use reason, and, in the end, we must stand by our informed consciences, regardless of where the issue stands in "popular opinion." If the Emperor is naked, we must be willing to say so, no matter the consequences.

A charge often brought against people who take issue with homosexual sexual activity is that these people are ignorant, intolerant, and hateful. This group is compared to those who opposed granting civil rights to people of diverse ethnic groups (an issue I will deal with later in this book).

Let me be very clear so that there is no misunderstanding. I do *not* hate people who engage in homosexual sex. Neither am I ignorant, uneducated, or secretly struggling with repressed homosexual desires. Normally, I would ignore such accusations. Objections like these are attacks on me as an individual rather than honest confrontations of my ideas. Although I am not a bigot, the ideas I present would be no less true or false even if I was. These ideas are either correct, or they are not. My character has nothing to do with it. Attacking me personally will not convince a reasonable reader that my argument is *necessarily* wrong.

Let me explain what I mean by introducing you to George and John. These two fellows will be with us at different points throughout the book to help me explain some of my points.

> **George:** "I have reviewed the evidence and I have concluded that stealing is wrong."
>
> **John:** "But George, everyone knows you are a bigot, and a hateful, conservative, Evangelical Christian. Therefore you

cannot possibly be correct in your conclusion."

George: "It is true that I am an Evangelical Christian, but you will need to prove that I am wrong by providing an argument that is better than my argument. Simply attacking my character does not prove that my conclusion is false."

In the same way, a charge of hate and bigotry against me does not prove anything about whether the arguments I make here are correct or not. Some may argue that I not *only* have a character flaw (bigotry), but *because* of that character flaw I have a bias. While I disagree about the particular character flaw, I readily admit a bias. That is to say, I believe, and believe strongly, in the truth of the statements I have written in this book. This does not mean I have not given these issues critical thought. Every reader is likely to have a bias as well. That is to be expected. All I ask is for each reader to subject the ideas in this book to critical thought. Try to analyze what you read without determining that these ideas are incorrect before you give them a chance. You are free to *assume* beforehand that all of my ideas are incorrect, so long as you confirm your assumptions by giving these ideas fair thought.

Because it may be important to some readers, I will address the issue of bigotry. I love people. I love people who practice homosexual sex. I love all people, period. It is from love, not ignorance, fear, or hate, that I have written this book. Jesus of Nazareth said that all the law and the prophets could be summed up in the two greatest commandments: that we are to love the Lord our God with all of our hearts, souls and minds, and we are to love our neighbors as ourselves (Matthew 22:37-40). I believe what Jesus Christ said is true. Because I believe this, I must try to be obedient to these great commandments.

First, I must love God. In order to do that, I must speak the truth. I cannot claim I love God and refuse to speak the truth. If I believe the things I write here are true, I cannot neglect to write them because of fear of what others may say about me, or even because of fear that I may hurt the feelings of others. It does not matter whether the things I write about upset my wife, my children, my parents, my siblings, my friends, my enemies, or me. I must do what is right.

This does not mean I should write the truth without doing my best to present that truth in love, compassion, and humility. I must present these ideas with love, because to love God also means to love His creation. All those who read these words are His creations, who He loves awesomely. I do not want to hurt anyone. I only want to help my readers by trying to write, and live out, truth. The truth about right and wrong must be searched for, found, and obeyed. Sometimes we may be called to suffer for the sake of truth. I suffer now, because my relationships with Cara and others cannot be complete, because of our beliefs. Make no mistake; it is not only people who believe homosexual sex is morally right who suffer. Those of us who love them, and disagree, suffer too.

In addition to loving God, I am called to love my neighbor as myself. All people are my neighbors. I am called to have the kind of love for each person that I want for myself. Of course, it must be the kind of love I want for myself when I am at my best, not my worst. I ought to treat others as I would like to be treated, but not in the way I would want to be treated when I am at my most self-absorbed. When I am in that state, I would like everyone to leave me alone, in my immorality, so I can continue to harm myself and do things my own way. I must love in the way I would desire for myself when I am not thinking selfishly; the kind of love that would require my neighbor to hold me accountable to be the best I can be, to do right, and live in righteousness, to sacrifice my desires that are incorrectly focused and disordered, and to train my desires to aim at truth, justice, mercy, and humility. I would not want anyone to treat me with less love than that, and I intend to treat my readers with that kind of true love.

The truth is, I do desire Cara's 'happiness,' but not at any cost. I want to live at peace with her, but not at any cost. My desire for Cara's 'happiness' is secondary to my desire for her spiritual and physical well-being. To be well is more important; it is much higher than to be 'happy.' Happiness is an emotion I hope everyone may feel frequently, when the feeling is present for the right reasons. But I want Cara, and others, to have true joy. True joy comes only through true fulfillment, and that is something that only comes from a life surrendered to the Truth.

Sometimes showing love can cause pain. But, there is a difference between causing harm and causing pain. It may be painful for a child to be physically jerked out of the way of a bus, but no reasonable person would spare the child that pain and allow her to suffer the true harm of being struck by the bus. Some pains are necessary to keep us safe from true harm. Sometimes loving your neighbor means causing him pain.

I would not want my neighbor to act as though something I was doing was right or good or even acceptable, if, in fact, what I was doing was none of these. I want to be spared the flattery, the social scruples, and the fake kindness that this type of 'love' shows. I want to be told to my face when I am aimed in the wrong direction. And, if my neighbor could do so, I would want to be pointed in the right direction. That is what I propose to do in this book. I want to love my readers by pointing them in the right direction.

Now notice how some of you flinch at that last paragraph. Terms like arrogance and vanity come to your mind as you describe the author of those words. Who am I to suggest that I could know what is right for anyone else? Who am I to suggest I could correct someone and point him in the right direction? I warn you to examine those emotions and analyze your thoughts, because some of you are doing the very same thing. As you react to those words, some of you are doing exactly what you are condemning. You believe I am *wrong* to assume I can know what is right for other people; you believe I *ought* to think differently. In other words, you believe you know what is right for *me*. Whether what you believe about me is correct or not, you cannot believe those things and be fair. If you believe I was wrong to write that paragraph, you must think it is okay to believe someone is wrong. If it is okay for you to believe I am wrong, it is okay for me to believe other people are wrong.

In fact, I am going to state that certain behaviors are wrong, objectively wrong. That is to say, they are wrong at all times and in all places, no matter how anyone *feels* about them. These ideas may be hard to tolerate. You may not like to read what I have written, but please do not abandon this book because you are offended that I am so arrogant as to assume I can know what is right. Because, if you are honest with yourself, you also think you know what is right.

It is possible you would honestly say that you do not know what is right, and that no one can know what is right. If you do not believe you know what is right, hopefully this book will give you some basis upon which to discover the moral law that binds and frees us all. If you are certain you are correct that no one can know what is morally right or wrong, you should have no fear in giving this book a fair reading. In the end, God will judge between you and me and Him, and we will all be responsible for the things we believed, the things we rejected, and the things we refused to give a fair read.

I want those who struggle with the issues in this book to know the Truth, to be free, and to have joy... *not to feel condemned.* I want to bring hope, not judgment. I am not rejecting anyone.

We are going to look at this issue and the arguments made in favor of homosexual sexual activity starting with what the Bible says about homosexual sexual activity. (Please do not at this point think that this book is going to be all about the Bible. Most of what is written in this book is not based on Bible verses but rather on things we can all relate to,

Christians and non-Christians.) Then we will look at the historical argument.

We will go on to look at the issue from the perspective of Natural Law and objective truth. Finally, we will deal with the issue of what it means to be a homosexual, and whether there are any alternatives to engaging in a homosexual lifestyle. There is hope, great hope.

CHAPTER 2

The Burden of Proof

In any argument, one side must carry the burden of proof. I am an attorney, so for me this concept is particularly important. In a trial, it is very important that both sides know who has the burden of proof. The burden of proof can be described as the principle that one side must *prove* his argument is correct, while the other side must *defend* against the arguments of the side with the burden.

In a criminal case, the burden of proof is on the prosecution. The prosecution must convince a jury that the defendant is guilty, 'beyond a reasonable doubt.' That is to say, the jury must believe the evidence is so strong against the defendant that no reasonable doubts exist in their minds. In most civil cases, the plaintiff must prove his case by a preponderance of the evidence. This means the plaintiff must show that the evidence proves it is more likely than not that the defendant has wronged the plaintiff. You have probably seen the statue of the blind lady holding the scales. Imagine those scales tipping ever so slightly in favor of the plaintiff. If the defendant can keep those scales equal, or tip them in her favor, then the defendant wins.

Regarding the issue of homosexual sexual activity, the burden of proof is on the side arguing that homosexual sex is morally right. The reason for this is that the moral argument *for* homosexual sexual activity is the new guy on the block. That is not to say that homosexual sex has not existed for a long time. What I am suggesting is that the great majority of people who have existed on Earth for all of recorded history (including the present) have believed that homosexual sex is immoral.

I will specifically address historical arguments attempting to justify homosexual sexual activity later in this book, but for now, it is enough that the reader understands that homosexual sexual activity has been considered morally wrong by almost all people, at all times, and in all places. This fact does not *necessarily* prove that homosexual sex is wrong. Large groups of people have been wrong about morality before. The fact that most people have always believed homosexual sex is wrong is not proof that homosexual sex is morally wrong. However, the fact that homosexual sexual activity has been almost universally considered immoral, does mean something. It means that the person arguing to justify homosexual sexual activity is the prosecutor of the case and the person arguing that homosexual sex is wrong is the defendant. All I am attempting in this book is to show that the arguments commonly used to justify homosexual sexual activity are not convincing. I do not have to carry the burden of proof.

Think of it like this. Those who believe that homosexual sexual activity is *wrong* are innocent until proven guilty. This is because homosexual sexual activity has existed throughout almost all of human history, and the great majority of those who have dealt with the issue, have decided that the evidence shows homosexual sexual activity to be morally wrong. If a person wants to justify homosexual sexual activity at this moment in history, it is his burden to prove that the activity is morally right. In other words, those who want to claim that homosexual sex is morally right must convince those of us who believe it is wrong.

Please do not think I am saying more than I intend. There is nothing necessarily negative about having the burden of proof. Prosecutors take defendants to trial all the time with a very difficult burden of proof, and they win. Plaintiffs sue defendants all the time, and they win. Discovering who has the burden of proof is not important because it begins by showing who has the better argument, but because it gives a framework for deciding what is true when the argument is over.

My intention is not to *prosecute* those who claim homosexual sexual activity is morally right, but to *defend* the idea that it is morally wrong.

CHAPTER 3

The Biblical Issue

It has been suggested by some that the Bible approves of homosexual sexual activity. Others have proposed that the Bible does not prohibit the activity. This chapter will deal with what the Bible does and does not say about homosexual sex.

I believe the Bible teaches with both truth and authority in all the issues it covers. However, I do not assume this belief is common to every reader of this book. Whether you believe in the truth and authority of the Bible or not, this chapter will point out what the Bible teaches about homosexual sexual activity.

For those who personally believe the Bible teaches with authority, this chapter may be all the persuasion you need. For others who believe the Bible has no authority over you at all, you may want to skip this section entirely, although you may find this chapter interesting. For those who think what the Bible says may be persuasive or helpful in determining the correct answer to a moral question, I encourage you to continue reading. I believe the Bible teaches with authority. This does not mean that I cannot be objective about what the Bible does or does not teach. In fact, *because* I believe the Bible teaches with authority, it is very important to me to discover what the Bible actually teaches. If you believed a book had the authority to show you how you should live, you would want to make sure you were quite right about what the book actually taught.

I will begin by listing the main scriptural references to homosexual sexual relations found in the Bible:

Old Testament

Genesis 19:4-7

Before they had gone to bed, all the men from every part of the city of Sodom—both young and old—surrounded the house. They called to Lot, 'Where are the men who came to you tonight? Bring them out to us so that we can have sex with them.'

Lot went outside to meet them and shut the door behind him and said, 'No, my friends. Don't do this wicked thing.'

Leviticus 18:22

Do not have sexual relations with a man as one does with a woman; that is detestable.

Leviticus 20:13a

If a man has sexual relations with a man as one does with a woman, both of them have done what is detestable.

Judges 19:20-23

'You are welcome at my house,' the old man said. 'Let me supply whatever you need. Only don't spend the night in the square.' So he took him into his house and fed his donkeys. After they had washed their feet, they had something to eat and drink.

While they were enjoying themselves, some of the wicked men of the city surrounded the house. Pounding on the door, they shouted to the old man who owned the house, 'Bring out the man who came to your house so we can have sex with him.'

The owner of the house went outside and said to them, 'No, my friends, don't be so vile. Since this man is my guest, don't do this outrageous thing.'

New Testament

Romans 1:18-32

The wrath of God is being revealed from heaven against all the godlessness and wickedness of people, who suppress the truth by their wickedness, since what may be known about God is plain to them, because God has made it plain to them. For since the creation of the world God's invisible qualities—his eternal power and divine nature—have been clearly seen, being understood from what has been made, so that people are without excuse.

For although they knew God, they neither glorified him as God nor gave thanks to him, but their thinking became futile and their foolish hearts were darkened. Although they claimed to be wise, they became fools and exchanged the glory of the immortal God for images made to look like a mortal human being and birds and animals and reptiles.

Therefore God gave them over in the sinful desires of their hearts to sexual impurity for the degrading of their bodies with one another. They exchanged the truth about God for a lie, and worshiped and served created things rather than the Creator—who is forever praised. Amen.

Because of this, God gave them over to shameful lusts. Even their women exchanged natural sexual relations for unnatural ones. In the same way the men also abandoned natural relations with women and were inflamed with lust for one another. Men committed shameful acts with other men, and received in themselves the due penalty for their error.

Furthermore, just as they did not think it worthwhile to retain the knowledge of God, so God gave them over to a depraved mind, so that they do what ought not to be done. They have become filled with every kind of wickedness, evil, greed and depravity. They are full of envy, murder, strife, deceit and malice. They are gossips, slanderers, God-haters, insolent, arrogant and boastful; they invent ways of doing evil; they disobey their parents; they have no understanding, no fidelity, no love, no mercy. Although they know God's righteous decree that those who do such things deserve death, they not only continue to do these very things but also approve of those who practice them.

1 Corinthians 6:9-11

Or do you not know that wrongdoers will not inherit the kingdom of God? Do not be deceived: Neither the sexually immoral nor idolaters nor adulterers nor men who have sex with men nor thieves nor the greedy nor drunkards nor slanderers nor swindlers will inherit the kingdom of God. **And that is what some of you were. But you were washed, you were sanctified, you were justified in the name of the Lord Jesus Christ and by the Spirit of our God** (emphasis mine).

What you read above is basically all that is said on the subject of homosexual sex in the Bible. It is mentioned only in a negative context in both the Old and New Testaments, and it is described as a perversion,[1] particularly in the first chapter of Romans where the apostle Paul describes the mindset that leads to the practice.

The arguments against the authority of these biblical passages usually run along two lines. The first type of argument deals with the passages in the Old Testament. This argument generally compares the ban on homosexual sexual activity with other Old Testament laws, such as the bans on eating shellfish or pork. The problem with this argument is it shows a lack of understanding of Old Testament law. There is a distinction between ceremonial laws and moral laws.

---

[1] Perversion – Turning something right into something wrong; tw isting something from straight to bent.

The ceremonial laws set the Israelites apart from other people as God's chosen people. Christians believe these laws were fulfilled by Jesus Christ and are no longer binding. The ceremonial laws are different than the moral laws, which remain active today. These moral laws were reaffirmed in the New Testament. In fact, in the New Testament, the moral laws were generally stricter. They applied not only to actions, but to the hearts and minds of individuals.

For example, Jesus Christ says:

You have heard that it was said, 'Do not commit adultery.' But I tell you that anyone who looks at a woman lustfully has already committed adultery with her in his heart.

In the New Testament, the moral law is not diminished. It deals with the heart of the individual and demands faithfulness not only to black letter rules, but to true love of God and neighbor.

The second argument is more likely to be directed at the New Testament passages. This argument generally focuses on language and context. The argument suggests that the New Testament writers were not referring to homosexual sex at all, or they were referring to it in a different context than we see it today.

Neither of these arguments is convincing. First of all, homosexual sexual activity is much older than the New Testament. To suggest that the practice is different today is to choose to be ignorant of history. The biblical writers knew what homosexual sex was, and they were likely aware of it in all of its forms, from the promiscuous to the monogamous.

As to the interpretation and translation of particular words in the Bible, such arguments are frequently presented when someone wants the Bible to have a meaning different than what it clearly teaches. I am not suggesting that interpretation and translation issues are not important. These issues are of great importance. They were of great importance to all of the men and women who have interpreted and translated the Bible for thousands of years. It is because translation and interpretation issues are so important that it is unlikely the words in the Bible have different meanings than the meanings they have been given.

The more direct answer to the scriptural reliability question[2] is this: those, like me, who believe the Bible is accurate, have already answered those questions. We believe the Bible is accurate. There is no point in trying to argue that mistakes were made that cause the teachings of the Bible to be questionable. These arguments have been answered many times.[3] If the Bible is mistaken, then the Bible would not have any authority.

This last sentence may sum up your view of the Bible. You may not believe the Bible has any authority at all. If that is the case, I would ask you to recall that this chapter is not here to convince you that the Bible teaches with authority. This chapter is about what the Bible actually teaches. Whether the Bible is correct about what it teaches would take another book.

---

[2] That is to say, the question of whether the Bible has come to us i n the form it was written. This would include questions about wh ether the correct manuscripts were included or excluded from th e Bible.

[3] *See* McDowell, Josh; *The New Evidence That Demands A Verdict Fully Updated To Answer The Questions Challenging Christians T oday.* (1999), Nashville, Lutzer, Erwin W.; *Seven Reasons Why Yo u Can Trust the Bible.* (2008), Chicago

The fact is that arguments about whether the Bible is reliable are sometimes dishonest. Those who make these arguments often do not personally accept the authority of scripture for themselves. The arguer generally says that homosexual sex is not *condemned* in the Bible. Upon the rebuttal of that argument, the arguer says the Bible does not really teach with authority. He says the Bible has been incorrectly interpreted, or the wrong books were included, or there was a conspiracy in the early church, or there is a conspiracy among certain Christians. In other words, the Bible teaches what these arguers want it to teach, and if it does not teach what they want it to teach, then it teaches nothing, or we cannot know what it teaches. These arguers are dishonest because they begin by arguing from the authority of the Bible, but when put to the test, they do not accept the authority of the Bible for themselves. If you do not believe the Bible has authority, then simply say so, and move on to argue from something which we both agree has authority. You cannot have your cake and eat it too.

What we have just looked at are the few references to homosexual sexual activity in the Bible, but that is not the complete answer to the question.

The full answer to the question does not come from what the Bible teaches about forbidding homosexual sex, but in what the Bible teaches about the *only* proper context for human sexual activity. The Bible teaches that there is only one proper sexual union: the union of a man and a woman within the context of a marriage relationship.

Biblical Sexual Relationship

The Bible does not only say negative things about sex. In fact, the Bible celebrates in great detail the proper design of sexual relationships within heterosexual marriage. Jesus Christ quotes Genesis, the very first book of the Bible, and says:

'Haven't you read,' he replied, 'that at the beginning the Creator "made them male and female," and said, "For this reason a man will leave his father and mother and be united to his wife, and the two will become one flesh?" So they are no longer two, but one flesh. Therefore what God has joined together, let no one separate' (Matthew 19:4-6).

Early in the biblical account, God made man. "The Lord God said, 'It is not good for the man to be alone. I will make a helper suitable for him'" (Genesis 2:18). After this, God made woman.

The apostle Paul writes the following in the New Testament book of First Corinthians:

> [E]ach man should have sexual relations with his own wife, and each woman with her own husband. The husband should fulfill his marital duty to his wife, and likewise the wife to her husband (1 Corinthians 7:2b-3).

The New Testament book of Hebrews states: "Marriage should be honored by all, and the marriage bed kept pure, for God will judge the adulterer and all the sexually immoral" (Hebrews 13:4 NIV).

I could go on, but here is the point. The Bible refers to sex positively only when it occurs within a marriage between a man and a woman. Any other sexual activity is immoral. The Bible does not have to list every possible form of sexual immorality for a reasonable person to see that the Bible approves of only one morally pure sexual activity: sexual activity between a married man and a woman.

Some may object here and mention the Old Testament instances of polygamy. There are at least two things to consider when thinking about polygamy as it applies to the ideas in this book. First, polygamy always takes place between a man and a woman. In this case a man has multiple wives but each wife is a separate marriage. Second, polygamy was not the Creator's design. The words of Genesis, stated again by Jesus Christ in the New Testament, are clear: "That is why a man leaves his father and mother and is united to his wife, and they become one flesh" (Genesis 2:24). The design was for a man and a woman to unite and become one flesh, not for a man to unite with other women also and become one flesh with them. This is one reason why there is a warning to the kings of Israel in the Old Testament: "He must not take many wives..." (Deuteronomy 17:17). A review of the history of Old Testament individuals who took multiple wives shows that polygamy equals big problems. It is not the design of God, in the Bible, for men to have many wives. The design is for a man and a woman to marry, and go from being two, to becoming one flesh.

There is another significant problem I want to address. There is a confusion often caused *by* Christians. This confusion is the idea that somehow homosexual sexual activity is morally worse than any other sexual activity other than sexual activity between a married man and woman. Let me be very clear here; there is *no such distinction* made in the Bible. Homosexual sexual activity is not any worse than adultery, fornication, or any other perversion of a biblically moral sexual relationship. A man who looks at a woman, other than his wife, with lust in his heart is not morally superior to a man who has sex with another man. Sin is sin. In fact, because sin is a matter of the heart, it is quite possible that a man who knows what is right, and still chooses to lust, can have an even more wicked heart than a man who is confused about what is right and wrong and has sex with another man because he believes he is in romantic love. Both men, according to the Bible, have sinned. The lustful man has no right to claim that his sin is less evil. God looks at the heart. We have all perverted God's plan, whether through immoral sexual activity, gossip, laziness, gluttony or any other type of sin. I am not suggesting that I stand above anyone as morally superior. I am a sinner, the worst of sinners, and I have been saved and forgiven only because Jesus Christ loved me so much that he died for me *in spite of* my sin and my rejection of His law and His love. I love Him because He *first* loved me.

Clear Conscience

Those who believe that the Bible is true are not convinced by the argument from a 'clear conscience.' I mean the argument that states 'my conscience is not affected by the fact that I engage in homosexual sexual activity, therefore, engaging in homosexual sexual activity must not be wrong.' Those who use this argument may even strengthen their point by adding that their consciences *do* tell them it is wrong to steal or kill or engage in other forms of wrongdoing.

The first chapter of the book of Romans (a portion of which is printed above) tells us that God can give us over to our sin. In other words, we no longer hear our consciences speaking, or, even worse, our consciences tell us what we are doing is acceptable. Therefore, the fact that you can engage in an activity and not feel bad about it does not mean what you are doing is morally right. Most of us, if we continue doing wrong, will hear our consciences less and less.

Final Thoughts on Scripture

As a Christian I realize there are things the Bible addresses and things it does not. In other words there are debatable matters and non-debatable matters. It is important to know the difference, or we will quickly become Pharisees.[4] Homosexual sexual activity is a non-debatable matter because the Bible speaks clearly. The Bible both forbids the practice of homosexual sex and sets out in detail the proper context for sexual relationships.

According to scripture, we must Love the Lord our God with all of our heart, mind, soul and strength, and love our neighbors as ourselves (Luke 10:27). If we believe the Bible is true, we must not only obey the Bible's teachings, but we must also defend the Bible because it is God's word, and we show love for neither God nor our neighbors when we choose to ignore what the Bible says.

---

[4] Pharisees were a group of leaders among the Hebrew people. Jes us Christ often criticized Pharisees because they taught the letter of the law but their hearts were wicked.

We must keep in mind that the Bible teaches us more about sexual relationships than just when they are or are not appropriate. The Bible teaches us that sexual relationships are temporal and earthbound. In other words, relationships are not mainly about sex. When we die, if we go to heaven, there will be no sex. It will be a state of love beyond sex, above sex. We will see what God's love truly is for us, and what our love will truly be for each other, both men and women, beyond and above sex.

Even so, while we are living here on earth we must analyze our choices. We must choose morally right actions. We cannot allow sin in our lives. The Bible *does not* condone homosexual sex. If a person wants to justify homosexual sexual activity, he must justify it on some other grounds.

One More Thing

"Wait a second!" some cry. "Jesus said 'Do not judge, or you too will be judged' (Matthew 7:1). So how can you judge homosexual sexual activity?" This statement Jesus made seems to be pulled out frequently when someone does not want her actions to be subject to scrutiny. For those who would use this argument, let me explain. Jesus was not suggesting that we could not make any judgments about what is right and wrong. Neither was He suggesting that we should not share our judgments about what is right and wrong with other people. In fact, in the same sermon where Jesus said 'Do not judge, or you too will be judged' (Matthew 7:1), he talked about murder and adultery. There are different meanings of the word judge in the English language. For instance:

"The *judge* sentenced me to jail."

"I cannot *judge* which is better, the blue dress or the pink one."

"You should not *judge* him just because he is poor."

"The umpire made a poor judgment call, I was safe at home."

In the Greek language (the language the New Testament was originally written in and translated from), there are three different words used for 'judge.' The first basically means to condemn. The second essentially means to evaluate or discern. The third usually means to settle a dispute. Jesus uses the first sense of the word when He says 'Do not judge, or you too will be judged' (Matthew 7:1). We are not to condemn. God is the only one who can condemn. However we are supposed to judge (discern, evaluate) our actions and the actions of others. Claiming that homosexual sex is morally wrong or claiming that it is morally right are both judgments. These judgments are not final condemnations of individuals. They are judgments about what kind of behavior is good and what kind of behavior is bad. We all make these kinds of judgments, all of the time. Any parent learns quickly that these types of judgments are necessary when raising a child. Can you imagine what would happen if parents thought the words of Jesus about judging meant they could not tell their children to not play in the street, or to not kick their little sisters? Judgments about right and wrong are not condemnations. Jesus simply was not talking about judging right and wrong behavior.

Jesus shared the truth in love. I want to do the same. I am not writing this book to shame people, or to act like I am better than anyone else. I want to explore what is true because Jesus of Nazareth also said, "Then you will know the truth, and the truth will set you free" (John 8:32).

CHAPTER 4

It's All Greek to Me: The Historical Argument

Some use history to justify homosexual sexual activity. That is to say, some try to justify homosexual sexual activity, in part, because homosexual sex may have been accepted in another culture at another time. Ancient Greek culture is often used to support the claim that homosexual sexual activity has been accepted as normal in the past. In fact, there was a time in Greek culture when homosexual sex was accepted. However, as with most claims, there is more to this story.

In ancient Greek culture, acceptable homosexual sexual activity took place between a grown man and a pubescent boy. These relationships reportedly took the following form: an older man would educate a boy while also engaging in a sexual relationship with the child. This relationship only lasted until the child reached manhood. When the boy could grow a beard, the older man would get married to a woman and have children. This does not mean homosexual sex did not occur in other forms among the ancient Greeks. However, this was the *accepted* form of homosexual sexual activity in ancient Greek culture.

The context in which homosexual sex was accepted among ancient Greeks bears little resemblance to the recent call for the acceptance of modern homosexual relationships. In fact, it was generally looked down upon for a man in Greek society to take a passive role in homosexual sex. Moreover, these pederastic[1] homosexual relationships did not lead to "marriage" between persons of the same gender.

---

[1]Pederasty – homosexual sexual activity between men and boys

It is, however, recorded that the Roman Emperor Nero "married" two different men. In one case he played the role of the bride. In the other instance he played the role of husband to a young man who resembled one of his concubines. It should be noted that this behavior was, by no means, universally accepted, in either Greek or Roman society. It may also be noted that both cultures are considered to have had major moral issues that led to their eventual downfalls.

Those who want to point to ancient Greek or Roman culture as evidence that homosexual sexual activity is morally right may want to move carefully. They may prove too much. If we are to believe that because a practice was acceptable in a particular society at a particular time, then the practice should be accepted today, we would also have to consider cannibalism, slavery, and genocide as candidates for moral acceptability. After all, each of these practices have far more substantial places in history, in terms of cultural acceptability, than homosexual sex. The advocate of the historical argument should also consider that, if we want to use other societies as examples of how we should live, then homosexual sex would have to be considered immoral, because historically, most of the people in most societies have believed homosexual sex was morally wrong

However, even if we ignored these serious problems with the historical argument, most of the evidence from ancient Greek and Roman sources about homosexual sexual relationships would only prove that we should accept pederasty. I do not believe that this is what those who promote this particular argument desire.

Recent History

Those who hold that homosexual sexual activity is morally right point to another historical event to support their view. In 1973, the American Psychiatric Association (APA) made the decision to remove homosexuality from their list of mental disorders. Some point to this event as scientific evidence that homosexual sexual activity is normal and healthy. Again, the facts of the real story show that this event did nothing to provide scientific grounds for believing anything about the morality of homosexual sex.

In the late 1960s, activist groups began to lobby the APA, demanding they remove homosexuality from their list of mental disorders. Some of this advocacy included threats, bullying and disruption, including taking over APA meetings. By 1973, the activists had gained enough support to get the APA to vote to remove homosexuality from their list of mental disorders. The vote was 58% for removal to 37% against removal. In the end, the decision was not based in science, but was a political move. Psychiatrist Dr. Ronald Bayer described the decision as follows:

> The entire process, from the first confrontation organized by gay demonstrators to the referendum demanded by the orthodox psychiatrists, seemed to violate the most basic expectations about how questions of science should be resolved.

> Instead of being engaged in sober discussion of data, psychiatrists were swept up in a political controversy. The result was not a conclusion based on an approximation of the scientific truth as dictated by reason, but was instead an action demanded by the ideological temper of the times.[2]

Homosexual activist Barbara Gittings said:

It never was a medical decision and that's why I think the action came so fast. After all, it was only three years from the time that feminists and gays first zapped the APA at a behavior therapy session to the time the Board of Trustees voted in 1973 to approve removing homosexuality from the list of mental disorders. *It was a political move*[3] (emphasis mine).

Dr. Charles Socarides, who was involved in the decision making process, called this decision "the medical hoax of the century."[4]

No matter what one believes about whether homosexuality is a mental disorder, it is clear that

---

[2] Bayer, Ronald; *Homosexuality and American Psychiatry: The Politics of Diagnosis*, (1987), Princeton; p. 3-4

[3] Katz, Jonathan Ned; *Gay American History*, revised edition (1992), Plume; p.427

[4] Socarides, Charles W. in Kronemeyer, Robert; *Overcoming Homosexuality*, (1980), New York; p. 5

scientific decisions (like moral decisions) should not be made based on the emotional outcries and bullying tactics of outspoken activist groups. Scientific decisions should be based upon sober and reasoned research.

I am not, by the way, advocating for a return of homosexuality to the list of mental disorders. I am not a psychiatrist nor am I concerned with labeling homosexuality as a mental disease. Whether people ought to engage in homosexual sexual activity is not a scientific issue. It is a moral issue.

We have now seen that removing homosexuality from the list of mental diseases recognized by the APA is not proof that homosexual sex is normal and morally good. The decision by the APA does nothing to answer the question: Is it morally wrong to engage in homosexual sex? Consider the following conversation between George and John.

> **George:** "John, I am sorry to hear that your wife left you."
>
> **John:** "Thank you for your concern George, I still can't believe she would leave me when I did not do anything morally wrong."
>
> **George:** "But John, you were having an affair with her sister."

John: "What's your point?"

George: "My point is that you were committing adultery. You clearly *were* doing something morally wrong."

John: "Oh George, you are sorely mistaken. You see adultery is not considered a mental disease by the American Psychiatric Association so, obviously, it can't be morally wrong to commit adultery."

History does not provide a basis for the claim that homosexual sexual activity is normal and healthy. With very few exceptions, homosexual sex is now, and has always been, considered morally wrong. This does not mean homosexual sex *is* morally wrong. A historical show of hands is not enough to prove that a behavior is morally right or wrong. The point is, once again, those who argue that homosexual sexual activity is morally right and healthy will have to justify the behavior on other grounds.

CHAPTER 5

A Short Introduction to Natural Law

The Natural Law, as used here, refers to the system of objective moral truth by which we all ought to live. By objective moral truth I mean there are some things that are right and some things that are wrong, objectively, whether or not any particular person believes they are right or wrong. Moral truths are objective in the same way mathematical truths are objective. In other words, things are right or wrong in the same way that two plus two equals four. Two plus two equals four no matter how many people believe it equals three or five.

Moral truths are not justified by how many people believe they are true. Even if we all *believed* it was morally right to murder, this would not *make* it right. Murder is wrong objectively, no matter how we may feel about that fact.

C.S. Lewis suggests that Natural Law is the reason we can argue as humans. Lewis writes, in the first chapter of his book, *Mere Christianity*, that we can argue only because we all agree that there are rules that govern our behavior. Without a common agreement that these standards exist, we could only "fight like animals;" we could not argue.[1]

We may be able to argue about whether particular standards apply to particular behaviors, but we all understand that standards exist. When you catch me in a lie, I either admit I was wrong, or I make some excuse for why it was okay for me to lie in this particular situation. We argue. I attempt to *justify* my behavior. I may say you were not entitled to the information I lied about. I may say that telling you the truth would have hurt your feelings, or I had promised someone else I would not reveal the truth to you, or I

---

[1] Lewis, C.S.; *The Complete C.S. Lewis Signature Classics.* (2002), New York; p. 15

thought I would get in trouble if I told the truth. What you will never hear me or anyone else say, is that I lied because lying is not morally wrong. You are not likely to hear people honestly say that your sense of right and wrong is silly and that they will go on telling lies as often as they wish for any reason or no reason at all.[2]

Consider the following conversation between George and John:

> **George:** "It is hard to enjoy playing board games with you John, because you are always cheating."
>
> **John:** "What do you mean?"
>
> **George:** "You are always stealing my tokens and moving my piece when I am not looking."
>
> **John:** "What is your point?"
>
> **George:** "My point is, it is wrong for you to do those things."
>
> **John** (laughing): "You must be kidding, there is no such thing as right and wrong!"

---

[2] Lewis, C.S.; *The Complete C.S. Lewis Signature Classics.* (2002), New York; Ch.1.

I doubt whether many of you have had a conversation like the one above. This is simply not the way people talk. If George accuses John of cheating, John is usually going to either say he was not cheating or say there was some reason for his cheating that excuses his behavior. John is not going to act as if there was no standard that governed proper behavior, because John knows, just as George knows, and just as you and I know, there is a standard for our behavior. Right and wrong exist. Everyone knows this, whether they admit it or not. The moral law, the Natural Law, is a set of rules we all understand.

Human laws are sometimes identical to the Natural Law and sometimes they are different. To show the difference between the Natural Law and human laws, think about driving a car. When we are on the highway and we see another driver traveling faster than the posted speed limit by five miles-per-hour, very few of us notice or care. I would guess that few people believe speed limits are perfectly in line with moral behavior or the Natural Law. Human laws can be somewhat arbitrary. However, human laws are certainly *related* to moral behavior.

It is obviously careless to travel at excessively high rates of speed, because such behavior puts you and your passengers (as well as other vehicles, and people on the road) in danger. Recognizing that driving at high rates of speed is dangerous may give us a *moral* rule, something like, 'a person should not drive at rates of speed which unreasonably increase the chances of damage to his life and property or the lives and property of others.' Or put more simply, "driving too fast is dangerous to people and property and therefore it is morally wrong."

I think most of us would agree that this is a moral rule. However, this rule does not determine the exact number of miles-per-hour we ought to travel. Every individual has a different level of experience and skill; most automobiles differ in their safety features and handling abilities. So, we argue. In this case, we argue through our representatives in the government and we come up with a *human* rule. Perhaps we agree to a 45 miles-per-hour speed limit on a particular road. Does this mean everyone now agrees that someone who breaks this *human* rule by traveling at 50 miles-per-hour is necessarily violating the *moral* rule stated above? Of course not.

There are cases where I think most of us would agree that someone is violating the *moral* rule. For instance, if we see a person driving 120 miles-per-hour on a 45 miles-per-hour road, I believe most of us would judge that the driver was violating the *moral* rule.[3]

No Moral Rules?

If there were no *moral* rules that we all understood, then there would be no point in reading this book. It is only those who suggest there are no moral rules who truly question the Natural Law. There is no point in arguing with these people. Their position provides no basis they can use to justify their actions or to condemn your actions. If you support the view that there are no such things as moral rules you are wasting your time here, and you are wrong.

Did those of you who believe there are no moral rules disagree with me when I said you were

---

[3] There are, of course exceptions. Perhaps the driver is driving a r elative to the hospital or the driver has, through no fault of his ow n, lost control of his vehicle. However, assuming there is no defen se, the driver is taking unreasonable risks with his life and proper ty and with the lives and property of others. That is *morally* wron g.

wrong? Do you believe that you are right and I am wrong? If so you do believe in at least some objective truth. At the very least, you believe it is objectively true that I am wrong in my statement.

I cannot convince individuals that anything in particular is wrong if they believe there is no such thing as right and wrong. To be consistent, such people would also have to believe there is nothing *morally* wrong with betraying their friends, kidnapping children, or murdering innocent people, because, in their view, no actions are *morally* wrong.

'Individual Conscience People'

There are some people who believe moral rules are real, but they believe these rules are unique to each individual. In other words, these people believe it can be wrong for one individual to commit murder, but not for another individual. We will call these people the 'individual conscience people.' The 'individual conscience people' are no more reasonable than the people who believe there is no such thing as right and wrong. In the view of the 'individual conscience people,' even though a person may have an individual conscience, that person has no authority to extend the moral rules of his conscience to any other person.

We should slow down here. What I mean is that an 'individual conscience person' believes something can be wrong for him, but he does not believe he can tell you the same thing is wrong for you. The 'individual conscience person' believes he has no authority or ability to judge the behavior of anyone else, nor does anyone else have the authority or ability to judge the 'individual conscience person.' Since I cannot know what your conscience says to you, and you cannot know what my conscience says to me, it appears, if we accept the argument of the 'individual conscience person,' we cannot have any *moral* rules that apply to all of us. Luckily for me, my individual conscience tells me the 'individual conscience people' are wrong, and since each of us must listen to our individual consciences I am free to disregard their arguments. Right?

The last conversation you read between George and John (the one about cheating at board games), which makes no sense to normal people, would not make any more sense if John had said his 'individual conscience' tells him 'there is nothing wrong with cheating.' George would still think it was wrong for John to cheat, and George would be right.

If there are standards for behavior common to all people, then there is something to argue about. If there are not, then we are wasting our time reading books like this one. How can we ever suggest that any behavior is wrong for someone else if the truth is that things can only be right or wrong for individuals?

Consider the following statement that John made as an 'individual conscience person' to his four year old son:

> **John:** "Little Johnny, I have an individual conscience that tells me *I* should not step out into oncoming traffic, but you are an individual with your own individual conscience. So, if your individual conscience tells you it is *morally* right for you, then go ahead. After all, who am I to judge your behavior?"

Such a statement would be entirely consistent with the beliefs of the 'individual conscience people.' But, the 'individual conscience people' would not make this statement, because fortunately, in practice, they know this view to be obvious nonsense. Anyone who tried to parent using this moral system would quickly have his children removed by the state, and for good reason.

Only Human Rules

Another view is that there are no *moral* rules we need to follow, not in our individual consciences or anywhere else; rather, we ought to follow only *human* made rules. Human rules are made by the people in power or by the voters in a democratic process. Of course, if human rules are *created* by humans (in other words, the rules do not exist unless particular people want them to), then this position is really no different than the idea that there are no moral rules at all.

Again, we need to take this argument slowly. What the "no *moral* rules people" are promoting is the idea that any rule is justified *only* by the fact that people, individually or as a group, *decided* it should be the rule. There is no higher authority than the will of the people in power to justify the rule. But, if the people in power are free to create or not create rules, to accept or reject any rule they happen to like or dislike, then there is no standard, other than our own likes and dislikes, by which we can judge any rule. Most of the people in Germany believed it was right to follow Adolf Hitler during World War II. If there was no higher justification for right and wrong than the whims of those in power, what business did the international community have in punishing the individuals who committed war crimes? After all, these individuals were simply following the 'lawful' orders of their superiors. Why is everyone up in arms about the killing of innocents in other countries, when those innocents belong to minority ethnic groups that the majority, or at least those in power, have decided to terminate? Why do we care about slavery, or tyranny, or the plight of oppressed women? All of these things are 'legal,' or have been 'legal,' under *human* law. But we do care. We are outraged when we see slavery, or oppression, or tyranny. Why? And why does it usually seem like the more morally good a person is, the more they are upset by these atrocities? The answer is the Natural Law. We all know evil when we see it.

Sometimes we ignore evil when it happens to benefit us. We may justify harming someone else even though we would never think that person was justified in harming us. Why? Because we are selfish. Because harming that person benefits us somehow. Human made rules, if they are not based on the Natural Law, will always be an attempt to benefit those who make these rules. There may be some 'good' rules made that way. We may all agree that we should not allow individuals to kill one another. Such a rule would be good for everybody. That is, until those in the majority decided people should not be able to kill other people in the majority, but killing people in the minority is acceptable, and therefore *legal*. How then could we stop this human law and save the individuals in the minority? We could not appeal to objective moral law, because, under this system of thought, there are no *objective moral laws* only *human* made rules. Why should the minority be protected if it does not benefit the majority?

I cannot ignore mentioning here a human made rule that does allow for this type of murder. Abortion is responsible for the murder of millions of the most innocent and vulnerable living human people. Very few people try to justify abortion by arguing that it is okay to kill babies because 'we have decided as a society' that killing babies is acceptable. Instead they say that babies in the womb are not yet people, or they say the right of a mother to end a pregnancy taking place in her body is a greater right than the right of her baby to life. What we see is that they do argue. They argue based on an understanding that murder is objectively wrong. They attempt to show, that in the case of abortion, murder is justified. They prove by their arguments that they know there are objective moral rules. In this case they show that they know that murder is wrong. They prove that they believe in the Natural Law. What basis do we have to argue against any evil rule without the Natural Law?

I know everyone reading this understands there is such a thing as right and wrong, good and evil. We have known this since the first time we witnessed harm caused to an innocent individual. Good speaks to us in our hearts when we see evil and when we do evil. It speaks to us in our own guilt over the harm we have selfishly caused other people, and in our shame because of the harm we have caused ourselves. God has created the universe with a law, this is the Natural Law you recognize when you see and do good and evil. To ignore the existence of the Natural Law is to give up, and cut ties with, a large part of what makes you a human.

No Truth

There are also those who say there is no such thing as truth at all. They say there is no moral truth or any other kind of truth. To these people I would simply ask...is *that* statement true? In order to claim there is no truth, a person would have to admit that at least the statement, "there is no truth," is true. Once he admits this statement is true he has destroyed his own argument.

> **George:** "There is no truth."
> **John:** "Is that true?"
> **George:** "Of course it is true."
> **John:** "If your statement is *true*, then there must be some truth."

Providentially, you are likely in the group of people who recognize the Natural Law. You recognize that there are clearly things that are right, and things that are wrong, things that are good and evil. We know these things by their consequences, and often, we seem to know them naturally. We tend to sense them without having to be taught. There seems to be something in our nature, from our youngest years, that reacts negatively when harm is caused to a person, or even an animal, for some selfish purpose of an individual. In fact, the *arguments* about whether homosexual sex is right or wrong are often Natural Law arguments from both sides.

I ask that you carefully attend to what I have written in the next several chapters. What I have written in these chapters is, by and large, accessible to those who believe in God and those who do not believe. The only common thread we must have is a belief in morality and a belief that the starting place for morality is that we ought to do no harm.

I think the most practical way to address the issue of homosexual sexual activity from a Natural Law perspective is to begin with the most common Natural Law arguments that claim homosexual sexual activity is morally right.

CHAPTER 6

My Dog Bowser

(Bowser's name has been changed to protect the innocent)

Do an experiment. Go and search on the internet for a discussion about whether homosexual sex is right or wrong. You may come across something like the following statement: "We see homosexuality in the animal kingdom, therefore it is natural and normal and good."

Here we have an argument based on Natural Law principles. In this case, the argument attempts to show that homosexual sexual activity is in harmony with nature. The full argument would have to be stated as follows:

1.   Whatever is natural for humans is normal and good.

2.   Whatever is natural for animals is natural for humans.

3.   Homosexual sexual activity is natural for animals.

4.   Therefore homosexual sexual activity is natural for humans.

5.   Therefore homosexual sexual activity is normal and good.

If the premises[1] of this argument are true, then the conclusion is clearly true. But are the premises true?

We will take these premises one at a time. The first premise is: Whatever is natural for humans is good. To make any sense of that statement we would have to use some kind of context and apply some kind of measure to the 'natural' activity.

---

[1] Premises – statements that build the argument (in this case, the statements labeled 1-3).

For instance, it is clearly natural to eat, and to eat is good. Eating is good for the body and taking care of our bodies is a good thing. However, 'eating is good,' is clearly not universal in *context*. We all know there are certain things that should not be eaten, like human flesh, or food that belongs to someone else. There is also a measure or quantity issue, because too much eating turns something good, into something bad. Eating too much is harmful to the human body. It makes the body overweight and prone to disease. It would be easy to simply say that eating human flesh or eating too much food is obviously *unnatural*, and therefore not 'good.' However, that would be *too* easy, because one would no longer be saying anything meaningful when one said 'whatever is natural is good.' What one would really be saying is 'whatever is good is good.' This is a circular argument. The arguer would be defining the word 'natural' to be only the things the arguer already considers good and then calling *those* things natural and therefore 'good.'

It is quite natural (meaning that there are those with a clear and powerful inclination or instinct for the action) for many people to eat too much. This is true for animals as well. My cat and my Labrador,

Bowser, are two portly examples of this truth. In fact, it seems that among those who have basically unlimited access to food, this 'natural' tendency to over eat is common. It is clear then to say, that what is natural in this sense, is not necessarily good.

The next premise in the argument states that whatever is natural for animals is natural for humans.[2] Again, there are serious problems with this premise. Animals do all kinds of things that do not seem to be natural or good for humans. For example: animals eat their young, eat their (or others) feces, throw their feces, and bite the heads off of their mates. Here I will save time and deal with the third premise together with the second.

The third premise is that homosexual sexual activity is natural for animals. There are animals who engage in homosexual sexual activity. However, based on some of the other behaviors of animals I have described (none of which would be natural for

---

[2] I will not, at this point, devolve into an argument about whether humans are simply the highest animals. I do not believe that to be the truth. However, it makes no difference to the argument. You c an, if you choose, simply read the premise as 'whatever is natural for *any other* animal is natural for the human animal.'

humans), using the behavior of animals to justify the behavior of humans is no more persuasive for the person trying to justify homosexual sex than it would be for the person who is trying to justify throwing his excrement at you. Let George and John explain:

> **George:** "John, what are you doing?!"
>
> **John:** "I am sniffing this fellow's anus; it is my way of introducing myself and getting to know him."
>
> **George:** "You are embarrassing me John; I don't think this kind man appreciates the attention you are giving to his backside."
>
> **John:** "George, this behavior is natural for dogs so it is obviously natural, normal, and good for me."

If my friend visits my home and sees my male dog Bowser attempting to romance the male dog next door, she may point out that Bowser's behavior shows human homosexual sexual activity to be quite normal; after all, such behavior clearly exists in the animal world, "just look at Bowser." Unfortunately, my friend cannot hold her position consistently, for when Bowser completes his transaction with the neighbor dog and proceeds to begin romancing my friend's leg, she rightfully draws back in horror at the dirty little creature. If my friend was to experience this assault by a human rather than Bowser, she would wisely contact the authorities and see that this individual was prosecuted. She would not make arguments justifying the behavior as normal and good just because Bowser shared a natural desire to engage in similar behavior. I submit she would respond in an equally horrified manner if she witnessed her neighbor in her yard consuming his feces or eating the smaller of his twin sons. You may find these examples distasteful, and you should. There are many 'natural' behaviors in the animal world that we know are wrong to engage in for humans. The bottom line is that arguments about animals prove too much. If homosexual sexual behavior is natural and good because some animals are known to engage in it, then throwing your feces and romancing the legs of your houseguests are natural and good for the same reason.[3]

---

[3] Please note that I am not here trying to say that homosexual sex among humans is the same thing as humans eating their feces or t

To be fair, this chapter has not proven that the animal behavior argument is not at *all* persuasive, but simply that it is no *more* persuasive than someone trying to justify any behavior in the animal kingdom as a behavior that should be accepted as normal and good when done by humans. Since I know many behaviors in the animal world would be wrong for humans, this argument is not very persuasive at all.

Once again, those who want to justify homosexual sexual activity will have to do so on other grounds.

---

heir young. I am only pointing out that 'natural' behaviors in the animal world are not necessarily 'natural' and good behaviors for humans.

CHAPTER 7

'Born This Way' and Personal Choice

Nature vs. Nurture

This chapter deals with another, related, Natural Law argument used by those who want to justify homosexual sexual relationships. This argument centers on the nature vs. nurture distinction. The advocates of this argument say something like the following:

1. Any status that a person is born with is natural and good and should not be discriminated against.

2. Homosexuality is a status with which some people are born.

3. Therefore, homosexuality is natural and good and should not be discriminated against.

Another form of this argument, for the person who wants to bring God into the equation, would say:

1. God would not have made me to be attracted to people of my own gender unless he desired that I should enter into homosexual sexual relationships with those of my own gender.

2. God did make me attracted to people of my own gender.

3. God only makes and desires what is good.

4. Therefore God desires for me to engage in homosexual sexual relationships.

There are two issues to analyze here. The first question is whether, in fact, people are 'born homosexual.' This is an issue that is part scientific and part spiritual. The second question is, if people are born homosexual, does that mean that homosexual sex is morally right?

The first issue is scientific in so far as it relates to genetic or physical characteristics of an individual that cause him to be attracted to other people of his own gender. As I write this book, the evidence for such physical or genetic causes is unproven. That is to say, there is no conclusive science that links homosexual attraction to any particular gene. Dr. Francis S. Collins, Director of The National Institutes of Health and former Director of the National Center for Human Genome Research (which became National Human Genome Research Institute in 1997) who oversaw the International Human Genome Sequencing Consortium said:

> "An area of particularly strong public interest is the genetic basis of homosexuality. Evidence from twin studies does in fact support the conclusion that heritable factors play a role in male homosexuality. However, the likelihood that

the identical twin of a homosexual male will also be gay is about 20% (compared with 2-4 percent of males in the general population), indicating that sexual orientation is genetically influenced but not hardwired by DNA, and that whatever genes are involved represent predispositions, not predeterminations."[1]

By contrast the heritability estimates for some other personality traits are interesting:

1. General Cognitive Ability (50%)
2. Extroversion (54%)
3. Agreeableness (42%)
4. Conscientiousness (49%)
5. Neuroticism (48%)
6. Openness (57%)
7. Aggression (38%)
8. Traditionalism (54%)[2]

---

[1] Collins, Francis S. *The Language of God, A Scientist Presents Evidence for Belief*, (2006), New York; p. 260

[2] *See Above* at p. 258

One may notice that each of these other traits is substantially more likely to be inherited than homosexual predisposition.

Christians and Predispositions

Earlier I said these chapters would be accessible to those who believe in God and those who do not believe. For those who do not believe, you may replace the word sin with the words 'doing wrong' in the following section. You may also replace the word temptation(s) with the words 'predisposed desire(s).' As far as the reference to the biblical fall you may choose to ignore it completely. It is important here that the Christian and the non-Christian have an understanding of this issue, which is why Christian language and ideas are used.

This issue is spiritual as it relates to predispositions toward sin. Believers in Jesus Christ believe in an event known as the 'fall of man.' This event is the reason sin exists and the reason sin so permeates our world. We believe the 'fall' literally tore the fabric of the universe and the world we now live in is broken. Because of this belief in the 'fall of man,' Christians believe we are born with a predisposition toward sin. Any particular person could be more or less predisposed toward any particular sin. One may have a real problem keeping himself from an attraction toward stealing from others, but have very little attraction toward killing others. Another may have an attraction toward gluttony, but no desire to gossip. We are not all tempted in every way, but we are all tempted because of "our own evil desire" (James 1:14). Christians believe someone could be born with a predisposition to be attracted to people of the same gender.

Choice

Whether people are born with homosexual sexual attractions is not, at this point, able to be answered with scientific certainty. But the answer to the 'born this way' argument does not depend on the answer to that question, because, homosexual sexual *behavior* is a *choice*.

Let me be clear here.

A person must *choose* to engage in homosexual sexual activity.

The fact that someone is *attracted* to a particular behavior does not *determine* that the person *must engage* in that behavior.

Think about the following example: A man is very hungry. He walks down the street and happens upon a pastry shop. There are several hot steaming pastries sitting on a table, next to a basket, outside the shop. Written upon a sign on the table, are the words, "Honor system: please take one and put a coin in the basket." The man sees that these pastries look delicious. He knows he has two more miles to walk before he gets home. He has no coin, but he is very hungry. He is aware that, if he takes a pastry, no one will ever know. The man is very *attracted* to the idea of taking one of the pastries. He believes that taking a pastry would make him very happy.

We all understand that the man was born with a need to eat. We will even assume he was also born with a strong *attraction* or *predisposition* toward stealing. Nevertheless we all can see that the man must make a *choice*. He must choose to do the right thing or the wrong thing. If he steals the pastry, the fact that he was hungry will not be a defense. It will be no defense that he was born with a predisposition toward stealing.

The man will have to deal with whether his action is right or wrong regardless of how he feels about it, how much he may have been attracted to engaging in it or how happy it makes him. No one ought to excuse the man just because he has a predisposition toward wrong behavior.

People do not do things they do not *want* to do unless they *have* to do them for some reason. We already know that those who participate in homosexual sex *want* to engage in the behavior. Whether the desire to engage in the behavior was born into them is not the issue. If homosexual sex is wrong, it is no defense to suggest that the *desire* to engage in the behavior is inborn.

We know people are born with predispositions toward all kinds of behaviors, including alcoholism, violent tendencies and anger problems, as well as attractions to good behaviors like kindness, empathy, and hard work. All of these predispositions make certain behaviors attractive to these people. No reasonable person (operating from an understanding of the Natural Law), believes that because he is *attracted* to getting drunk all the time, or being violent toward another person, or giving vent to his anger whenever that happens to please him, that those actions are morally right. I am not comparing an attraction toward homosexual sex with any other particular attraction toward any other behavior. In other words, I am not stating that being violent or stealing is the same thing as having homosexual sex.

There is nothing morally wrong with having an *attraction* toward a particular action. What we *choose* to do with our attractions reveals our moral character. I am more attracted to selfishness than I am to kindness. My attraction to selfishness does not make me an immoral person. It is when I *choose* to act selfishly rather than with kindness that I am acting immorally. We all ought to encourage the right kinds of attractions in ourselves. We all ought to work to rid ourselves of the wrong kinds of attractions. But, we are all responsible for our *behavior.* Homosexual sex is an action. It is a behavior. People are morally responsible for their behaviors. Whether this behavior is morally right or morally wrong is what we must discover.

It should be noted here that the status of a person who chooses to engage in particular behaviors is not the same as the status of a person who is born with a particular hair color, skin color, born in a particular country, or born with a physical disfigurement. Such people are born with a *characteristic;* their *chosen behaviors* are still governed by the same Natural Law that governs all human beings.

Dr. Martin Luther King Junior said "I have a dream that my four little children will one day live in a nation where they will not be judged by the color of their skin, but by the content of their character."[3] He made an important distinction. He believed people should not be judged by the *characteristics* they were born with, but by the *actions* they *chose.* Dr. King did not want people to be judged based upon things they can do nothing about and have no control over, but he did want people to be judged based on their character, based on the behaviors they chose. This is why homosexual sexual activity is not a civil rights issue. I would stand with anyone who said people should not discriminate against others simply because they were born with an *attraction* for people of their same gender. To discriminate based on predispositions is

---

[3] King, Martin Luther Jr. *I Have a Dream: Writings and Speeches t hat Changed the World.* Ed. James M. Washington. (1992) San Fr ancisco

clearly wrong. The Natural Law speaks plainly on this issue. However, people are responsible for what they *choose* to do with their attractions.

Racial Bigots

There is a major difference between a racial bigot and a Christian who believes homosexual sex is wrong. Racial bigots dislike people because of the color of their skin. Christians do not dislike people (or, at least, they ought not to dislike people) just because those people have a predisposition toward being attracted to other people of their own gender. Christians do not even dislike people who *engage* in homosexual sexual activity. Christians love people. Christians simply believe that the *action* of having homosexual sex is wrong. They love people.

Some people have grown tired of the 'love the person, hate the sin' attitude. I understand the frustration. However, we must admit we all have this attitude in one way or another. You love your friend, but you hate that she is undependable. You love your brother but you hate his anger problem. You love your uncle Jack but you hate the fact that he is always gossiping. To love someone, but not approve of her morally wrong actions is normal and healthy. It shows you care not only for her, but you want her to be the best she can be.

Once again, homosexual sexual activity must be justified on grounds other than the possible fact that *attractions* to homosexual sexual *behavior* may be inborn.

CHAPTER 8

"Who Are You to Tell Me?"
Two Views

In this chapter we will look at another class of argument I call it the libertarian/relativistic argument. I name the argument this way because the argument can be used from either a libertarian or a relativistic worldview. We will deal with both. This argument normally takes the form: 'Who are you to tell me what I can do with my own body?'

Mind Your Own Business

Before we analyze this argument from the libertarian and relativistic worldviews, I want to point out that, depending on how this argument is used, the argument suffers from a logical fallacy. This fallacy is sometimes called the Mind Your Own Business Fallacy. The Mind Your Own Business Fallacy tries to stop any discussion of a person's behavior, no matter how immoral the behavior may be, by claiming the behavior is private and therefore irrelevant to those who are not involved. An example can be found in the statement, 'So what if I was smoking crack around my child in my apartment, how does that affect you?' Or the similar statement, 'Why do you care if I beat my wife in our own home? It isn't any of your business.' Again, I am not saying that smoking crack or beating one's wife is the same as having homosexual sex. I am just pointing out other forms of the Mind Your Own Business Fallacy. The argument is regularly made in the form: 'Why do you care if two consenting adults have homosexual sex in the privacy of their own home?' Or, 'How does my homosexual "marriage" affect you?' The reason the Mind Your Own Business Fallacy is an improper argument is because statements like the ones above *cannot justify the behavior being discussed.* Instead, the statements try to end the argument by suggesting that the person who claims the behavior is immoral has no right to make that claim because, supposedly, the behavior is not affecting him personally.

The problem is that if it was true that no one could make a moral judgment about behavior *unless* it affected him personally, then you could not claim that *any* behavior was immoral until it affected you. You could not believe murder was wrong until you yourself, or someone you loved, was murdered. You could not claim adultery was wrong for anyone but your own spouse. You could not claim stealing was wrong unless someone stole from you. Consider the following conversation between George and John.

> **John:** "George, have you seen this article? There are people in Australia who are trying to make child prostitution legal."
>
> **George:** "There's nothing immoral about that."
>
> **John:** "Why not?"
>
> **George:** "Because my children don't live in Australia."

At this point you may be thinking that some of the examples used above are not the same as homosexual sex. After all, the type of homosexual sex we are talking about takes place between two consenting adults. How is that like beating one's wife or child prostitution? My answer is simple. It is not. However, that is not the point. This argument contains a fallacy because it tries to end debate on a moral issue by artificially making it a private issue. The argument states that because a particular behavior is not affecting you personally, you are not allowed to make a moral evaluation of the behavior.

To be fair, there are probably some people using the 'who are you to tell me what I can do with my own body' argument who are not using it to show that their behavior is morally right. These people may actually be saying that, whether or not the behavior is in fact immoral, you do not have the right to control the behavior. We will deal with that form of the argument next.

Libertarianism

In the criminal law there are crimes of commission and crimes of omission. This means there are crimes you can commit by *doing* something, like stealing or kidnapping, and crimes you can commit by *not doing* something you were supposed to do, like child neglect or failure to report knowledge of a terrorist act.

There are very few crimes of omission in English common law. A classic example, that has horrified morally sensible students of the law for years, is the story of the drowning man. This example usually takes the following form:

> John walks by a swimming pool and witnesses George drowning. George is shouting and pleading for help. John could easily save George with no danger to himself by tossing George the life preserver, which is sitting at John's feet. John ignores George and continues to walk by as George, finally exhausted, surrenders to his fatigue and dies.

Under the English common law John is not guilty of any crime. Most of us however, see John's failure to rescue George as a major moral failing. We see it as wrong. But John has not done anything illegal. This story provides a good illustration of the difference between the minimum standard the law requires and the standard to which a moral person ought to hold herself. As we look at the 'who are you to tell me what I can do with my body' argument, keep this distinction in mind. There are some things which are technically legal to do, but are nevertheless incredibly immoral.

The libertarian form of the 'who are you to tell me what to do with my own body' argument appeals to the Natural Law principle that freedom is usually good, and unnecessary restrictions are usually bad.

First Things First

First, we must get a critical issue out of the way. We must realize that, whether or not this argument is correct, the libertarian form of this argument cannot show whether homosexual sexual activity is moral or immoral. This is because this argument only deals with whether or not one human, or set of humans, can tell other humans what kinds of things they are allowed to do. It cannot settle the issue of whether the specific things people do are morally right or wrong.

If the libertarian form of the argument proved that I, or the government, or some other ruling body, had no right to tell someone they could not eat more than 2000 calories a day, that conclusion would not tell us anything about whether it was right or wrong to eat more than 2000 calories a day. It would only clarify the person to whom the human is responsible. It might show that instead of answering to me, you only must answer to the state, or, instead of answering to the state, you only must answer to yourself, or to the Natural Law, or to God.

This is an issue of jurisdiction.[1] This is not an issue of the morality of the behavior being discussed. That is to say, the issue raised by this argument is, whether it is morally right for me to *tell* you that you ought not to engage in homosexual sexual behavior, or you ought not to 'marry' someone of the same gender. The issue is *not* whether homosexual sexual behavior or redefining marriage are morally right or wrong. Perhaps George and John can make this clear.

George: "John, you need to stop viewing pornography."

---

[1] Jurisdiction – Authority to speak the law.

> **John:** "Who are you to tell me what to do?"
>
> **George:** I am just telling you that you should stop, because viewing pornography is immoral."
>
> **John:** "Maybe viewing pornography is morally wrong and maybe it isn't. Either way you have no business trying to control my actions."

John has made the 'who are you to tell me what to do with my own body' argument in its libertarian form. John is not trying to justify the morality of viewing pornography; he is simply claiming George has no jurisdiction to *tell* him what to do. I am not especially concerned with the libertarian form of the argument in this book. I am writing about whether the act of homosexual sex is morally right or morally wrong, not whether any person, or group of people, has the right to control that behavior.

However, because the government's legal recognition of homosexual "marriage" is a real issue for the reader, it is worthwhile to analyze the argument and examine its merits.

We will begin with our responsibility to individuals. I do not have the jurisdiction to outlaw homosexual sex or homosexual "marriage." I am not the government and I have no power to create any law for the public at large. I cannot decide what speed drivers can go on a public highway, nor can I even tell others they may not steal from one another. I have neither the police power to enforce any public law, nor the consent of the public to create any law. My jurisdiction is limited.

The government, however, does have the *power* to make almost any law. This does not mean the government has the *right* to make any law. For instance, I think we would all agree that the government does not have the *right* to make a law mandating that all parents must give their firstborn children to the government as a tax. The *right* of the government to make any law is limited by morality. The government has the *power* to enforce a law like the example above by physically taking my firstborn child, but such a law would be immoral and therefore outside the government's limited jurisdiction. This idea has been at the heart of all reasonable systems of government since the rejection of the doctrine of the divine right of kings.[2]

There is no question that the government is limited to making laws it has the moral right to enforce. Therefore, the question becomes, is it immoral for the government to tell us what we can do with our own bodies? We will look at three examples where the government does that very thing: suicide, drug use, and abortion.

In the first example, suicide, the government says a person cannot commit self-murder. This is an interesting example because if the criminal is successful, the government is unable to prosecute the crime. Nevertheless, the government asserts that human life has value; therefore a person may not destroy his own life.

Drug use is an example where the government is making a moral conclusion that damaging one's body, and chemically altering one's mind in certain ways, are immoral actions. There are certainly other

---

[2] The doctrine of the divine right of kings suggested that only God could judge the king. Therefore the king's power was complete an d unquestionable. The king could make and enforce any law he c hose.

possible reasons to ban drug use, such as the level at which drug use appears to lead to other crimes, or the degree to which drug use makes a person less likely to be a productive member of society. However, an argument can be made that there are people who could use drugs recreationally and not necessarily commit other crimes or become bad citizens as a result.

In the case of abortion, the American government says that, past a certain point of pregnancy (depending on where one lives), a woman may not abort the child who is living and growing in her body. This example is particularly difficult because most people believe (although they may differ as to the time frames involved) that two bodies are involved: the woman's and her baby's. However, in this case, the government is dictating what a person must not do and what a person must do. The government dictates what the woman *must not* do by saying a woman may not abort the baby, and what she *must* do by saying the woman must go through the process of giving birth.

Here comes the point. Whether you believe the government has the right to mandate all of these specific things, or none of them, the underlying principal is correct. The government has the right to dictate what a person may do with her body when the activity being banned or mandated has particularly serious moral consequences. This does not necessarily mean the government *must* make these laws, but it does show the government has the *right* to make these laws, if the laws can be justified on moral grounds. To believe otherwise and take the concept to its logical libertarian end (by which I mean the government could not make any laws governing the behavior of individuals as to their own bodies) would be to allow all kinds of harm in society.

The libertarian form of the argument states that government should not make laws *telling* people what they can do to themselves, as long as what they are doing is not affecting other people. However, it is simply not true that any of the things listed above can be done without affecting other people. Anyone who has had a drug abuser in his family or a relative who has committed suicide can testify to the serious and often very painful effects these behaviors have on other people. We live in a social society, a social world. The actions we take affect other people.

Again, it comes down to whether or not homosexual sexual relationships are moral. If homosexual sexual behavior is morally justified, the government would have the right to recognize the relationships of those who want to engage in homosexual sex. If homosexual sexual relationships are immoral, it is likely that the government would have the right to ban homosexual sex and refuse to recognize homosexual relationships, as to do the opposite might be to approve of immoral behavior.

I want to make one more point here. I am not intending to debate the merits of libertarianism generally. I respect the political philosophy of those who believe government should interfere as little as possible with the lives of the people. For those who hold this view, it may be consistent to also hold that homosexual sex and homosexual "marriage" should not be the concern of the government. Again, the libertarian argument does not assist us in discovering whether homosexual sexual relations are morally right or wrong; if the argument is correct it would only show that the *government* should not be involved in the question at all. However, to be truly consistent, a person who held this view would also have to believe that the government should not be involved in the issue of heterosexual marriage either. The government should either ignore issues like marriage altogether, or the government should be able to decide whether recognizing certain types of unions is immoral. We cannot have it both ways.

It is possible that some of those who use the 'who are you to tell me what to do with my own body' argument are not truly libertarian in their political theory, but, they want to adopt a libertarian political philosophy only for the specific issue of homosexual "marriage." This is an inconsistent position to hold because libertarianism is not a buffet from which people can choose individual issues. If George wants to use libertarianism to justify entering a homosexual "marriage" then John can use libertarianism to justify entering a "marriage" with his biological sister, or to use crack, or to kill himself. In other words, libertarianism is either the correct philosophy for governments to follow, which means governments must not involve themselves in these types of moral questions, or libertarianism is not the correct philosophy, in which case governments may involve themselves in these types of moral questions. You are either a libertarian or you are not.

Relativism

Now we will look at the 'who are you to tell me what to do with my own body' argument in the context of relativism. In this context, the sentence 'who are you to tell me what I can do with my own body' has a different justification.

The libertarian argument would agree that there is an objective system of morality,[3] and would simply say that one of the rules of the objective system of morality is that it is immoral for certain people or entities (like a government) to *enforce* some kinds of moral rules against other individuals. The relativist form of the argument states that there are no *objective* morals for the community at all. Therefore, one person cannot tell another what to do, because, from this viewpoint, each individual is the sole dictator of her own morals. In other words, the relativist does not just say 'you should not tell me what to do because you do not have the right to tell me what to do,' he says 'you

---

[3] *See* Chapter 1

should not tell me what to do because there is no such thing as a true moral rule that applies to everyone.'

The relativist may say something like: 'Well that may be wrong for you but it is not wrong for me.' What he means is that there is no standard set of morals every person must follow, but rather some sort of completely individual conscience that each person possesses and uses to make or understand rules for himself. One person's rules would not necessarily apply to any other person.

We dealt with some of these issues in chapter five, but, because the same issues appear again in the context of this argument, I will address this view.

If the people who advocate this view are correct, then who are *they* to say that *I* cannot enforce rules upon others? If it is the rule of my individual conscience to tell others what to do with their bodies then, according to the relativist's system, I should be free to live out that rule. Read this conversation between George and John.

> **George:** "John, you should not be so lazy, it's morally wrong to act that way."
> **John:** "Who are you to tell me what to do?"

George: "What do you mean?"

John: "You can't know my heart and you can't know what is in my conscience."

George: "That's true, but what does that have to do with you being lazy?"

John: "My conscience tells me that being lazy is good. You can't tell me that being lazy is bad because I only have to follow my conscience."

George: "Let me ask you a question, John. If your conscience tells you to do something, would it would be wrong if you did not do that thing?"

John: "Of course, I have to follow my conscience. Doing what my conscience tells me is what is right for me."

George: "Well John, I have a problem with your moral system."

John: "What problem do you have?"

George: "When I told you that laziness was immoral I was following my conscience."

John: "What do *you* mean?"

George: "I mean that my conscience told *me* that I should *tell you* that laziness is immoral. Don't I have to follow my conscience?"

John: "I do think you should follow your conscience but I don't think you should tell other people that they are wrong."

George: "I am sorry John, perhaps you're right, but, just so I am clear on the rules, you are saying that it is wrong to tell other people they're wrong."

John: "Yes, you should not tell other people that they are wrong because you can't know what is in their conscience."

George: "John, don't you realize that when you tell me that I am wrong to tell other people they are wrong you are doing exactly the same thing you are telling me not to do?"

John: "No I'm not."

George: "You are telling me it's wrong to tell people they are wrong, correct?"

John: "Yes."

George: "So I am wrong?"

John: "Yes...Oh I see."

George: "...John."

John: "Yes George."

George: "You should not be so lazy, it's morally wrong to act that way."

As John shows us, the relativist will likely argue that I am allowed to have an individual conscience so long as the things my conscience tells me do not involve controlling the behavior of anyone else. The reasonable reply to this would be: 'Is the rule that my individual conscience should not affect anyone else an *objective* moral rule or just another of the rules in *your* individual conscience? Because, if it is just one of the rules in your individual conscience, I have no duty to obey that rule, and if it is an objective rule then you are admitting that there is some standard of behavior which we all must obey? Therefore *you* are now telling *me* what to do. And, by the way, what proof do you have that this particular rule about not affecting others is the *only* objective rule we must obey. After all, such a rule is convenient only for those whose individual consciences do not require them to affect others.' Consider another conversation between our friends George and John.

George: "John, I have been thinking. My conscience tells me it is wrong to seduce another man's wife."

John: "I don't know George; my conscience tells me adultery is fine as long as the person I am seducing is very attractive."

George: "John, I think you are wrong about that. Adultery is always wrong"

John: "For you perhaps, George, but not for me."

George: "No, I believe it is wrong for you also."

John: "Now hold on a minute George, who are you to tell me what to do with my own body?"

George: "What do you mean?"

John: "I mean, you cannot tell other people something is wrong for them just because your conscience tells you the thing is wrong for you."

George: "But my conscience tells me adultery is not just wrong for me. My conscience tells me it is wrong for everybody, including you John."

John: "No, no, no my friend, you have it all wrong. Let me explain. Your conscience is allowed to tell you what is wrong for you but not what is wrong for anyone else. That is the only rule you know."

George: "I think I see your point, I guess I will have to rethink my view on this issue."

John: "Good man, I am glad you have seen the error of your ways."

(One minute later...)

George: "I have been thinking."

John: "Yes George."

George: "My conscience tells me that adultery is okay too, as long as the person I am seducing is your wife. After all, if she wants to, who am I to tell her what to do with her own body? Thank you for this lesson."

The relativist cannot have it both ways. If one's individual conscience is the only moral guide, then the relativist cannot make statements like 'who are *you* to tell me what to do with my own body?' These kinds of statements are judgments themselves. Neither can the relativist support the supposed rule, 'no person's individual morals should control anyone else,' because the relativist cannot show a reasonable basis for how he has arrived at the conclusion that this is the *only* objective moral truth.

The fact is that there *is* a universal system of objective moral standards, and most arguments which try to justify homosexual sexual activity attempt to use that objective system of morality to justify the behavior, as has been pointed out in the arguments we have looked at so far. So, again, the moral justification for homosexual sex will have to be proven on some other grounds.

CHAPTER 9

<u>Do No Harm</u>

"One should do harm to no man."

St. Thomas Aquinas

The principle that we ought to do no harm is fundamental to the Natural Law. The idea that people should not harm themselves, others, or nature is at the foundation of how reasonable people ought to understand morality. In this chapter, we are going to build a framework for what it means to 'do no harm.'

We need this framework so we can determine whether homosexual sexual relationships are, in fact, harmful, and whether people are doing harm to themselves, others, or nature when they take part in homosexual sexual relationships. Simply put, if these relationships cause harm, then homosexual sex is morally wrong.

The Definition of Harm

In order to understand what we mean when we say do no harm, we first need to know what 'harm' means. Here is the definition of harm from dictionary.com:

harm – noun

1. physical injury or mental damage; hurt: to do him bodily harm.

2. moral injury; evil; wrong.[1]

The first definition talks about harm in terms of injury and damage, while the second talks about harm in terms of moral harm and evil. The second definition does us no good here since we can only talk about

---

[1] http://dictionary.reference.com/browse/harm?s=t last visited April 30, 2013

---

moral harm and evil when we have discovered what moral right and good are.

Looking then to the first definition, we see that physical injury and mental damage are listed as harms. But, we know instinctively that these things are not always harms in the moral sense of the word. For instance, if we have surgery to remove cancer cells we realize the surgery causes a physical injury to our body, but no reasonable person believes we have been harmed in the moral sense of the word.

> **John:** "George, I just got out of surgery and the doctors say they got all the cancer!"
>
> **George:** "Well John, you sound very pleased, I am glad you can still be so happy when, according to my dictionary, you have received a physical injury from the surgeon's incision and have therefore been harmed."

This conversation sounds ridiculous because it is ridiculous. The fact is that we cannot easily define the word harm, in its moral sense, because harm is really just the opposite of good. You may now be thinking 'I thought evil was the opposite of good.' You are correct. Evil is the opposite of good. Evil can only be understood when we know what *good* is. In the same way we cannot know what *harm* is unless we know what *good* is.

Here is what I mean. If we take the example we used earlier of a person having surgery to remove cancer, we have to look at what the *good* is and what the *harm* is. It does not take much argument for most people to see that life is a *good* and death is a *harm*. In the same way we can also see that a pain-free body is a *good* and a damaged body that is in pain is a *harm*.

In this example we have two *goods* and two *harms*. Our first good is keeping a pain-free body and our second good is staying alive. John's choice of harms in the above example is either: having a surgery which causes damage and pain to his body, or not removing the cancer and dying. So, in this example, John has to experience bodily damage and pain in order to avoid death. Since we naturally know that dying is a greater harm than physical injury, we can agree that having surgery, in this case, is a *good*. Does that mean the bodily damage and pain caused by the surgery are not truly harms? In the moral sense of the word harm, they are not. This brings us to the definition of harm we are using here. The definition of harm, in a moral sense, is more like the second definition from above than like the first one. When we say 'do no harm,' we mean literally do no wrong, no moral harm, no evil.

But earlier I wrote "the second definition does us no good here since we can only talk about moral harm and evil when we have discovered what moral right and good are." So how can I now say the second definition is the one we are, in fact, going to use? Let me explain. It is true that we cannot know what it means to 'do no evil' if we do not know what evil is, and we cannot know what evil is unless we know what good is, because doing evil is doing what is not good. The first definition of harm was helpful because it gave us an idea of what some kinds of evil are. Physical injury and mental damage are often evil. As we have seen, however, sometimes it may actually be *good* to cause physical injury if the good to be gained from the physical injury is a greater *good* than the *evil* or *wrong* we would achieve by not causing the physical injury.

Lesser of Two Evils?

John: "Who are you voting for in the big election?

George: "I am going to vote for candidate Fancypants. How about you? Who are you going to vote for?

John: "I don't want to vote for either candidate. They are both evil."

George: "Of course they are evil. Everyone knows that. You simply must try to choose the lesser of two evils."

People seem to have conversations like the one above every time there is a major political race. Whether or not George is correct in his political theory, this example illustrates one common situation where people try to make distinctions between lesser and greater goods and evils. In order to understand what moral harm is, we must understand what we mean when we talk about choices between different goods and evils.

Pleasure over Pain

There are those who have suggested that a simple equation of the type we are discussing is the *only* thing we need to think about when deciding what is right and what is wrong. These people suggest that whatever moral choice causes the *most* pleasure and avoids the *most* pain is the right moral choice. For them, pain is evil and pleasure is good.

While this type of moral decision making may happen to lead to correct moral judgments some of the time, it is not a proper way to think about morality. For example, it is true to say that for John to have surgery to remove cancer is a small pain, but the small pain will save his life, which means that John will get to have many more pleasures (because he will live longer). In fact, John will likely get to have many more pleasures, and they may outweigh his pain in having surgery. But that is not the reason that the surgery was the right moral choice. John's surgery is the right moral choice because he chose *life* over pain. We could not possibly know whether John's life after surgery will be filled with pleasure rather than filled with pain. Some lives are filled with pain. This shows us the first problem with pure 'amount of pain versus amount of pleasure' moral reasoning. The problem is

that we cannot truly measure the amount of pain or
pleasure involved when making these moral decisions,
because such measurements are impossible most of the
time. The second problem with this type of moral
reasoning will be shown in the following conversation
between John and George:

John: "George, I have discovered a method
that allows me to always know what is
morally right and what is morally wrong!"

George: "By all means sir, tell me at once,
so that I too may know what is morally
right and morally wrong."

John: "My method is simple: you calculate
the amount of pain or pleasure caused by
each possible moral choice and you choose
the action which causes the most pleasure
and the least pain."

George: "Brilliant John, if that method
works it will revolutionize the way we
think about morality."

John: "Thank you George."

George: "But does it work?"

John: "What do you mean? Of course it works! Can't you see that in every case the moral choice I make will cause the most possible pleasure and avoid the most possible pain?"

George: "Oh certainly, I can see what you say is true, but will such a moral equation always produce the result that is morally right? Can you give me an example?"

John: "Absolutely, all you have to do is weigh pleasures and pain. Think about this: If I had the choice of receiving a slap on the hand, and because I received that slap you would receive $10,00.00, it would clearly be the morally right thing for me to do to receive the slap."

George: "Why is that?"

John: "Because if we measure the pain I would receive from a slap on the hand, which would be very little pain indeed, and the pleasure you would receive from gaining $10,00.00, which would be a good deal of pleasure, we can see that my small sacrifice for your great gain is the morally right choice for me."

George: "I think I see your point, I would surely derive much pleasure from receiving $10,00.00 and the pain to your body would certainly be small. I think you may have solved the moral problems of the world with this idea. But does it work every time?"

John: "It must, it just makes sense."

George: "Do you mind if I try an example?"

John: "Please do sir."

George: "Let's say we use your 4 year old son, little Johnny, for our example."

John: "Alright, how shall we use him?"

George: "I will show you. Let's say that we have the following choices: If we make the first choice, everyone in the world, close to 7 billion people, will receive $10,00.00, if we make the second choice no one will receive anything."

John: "That would cause a lot of pleasure indeed! What are our choices?"

George: "The choices are simple. If we allow little Johnny to be horribly tortured for ten years, everyone will get the money, but if we spare little Johnny the torture, no one will get the money."

John: "That is terrible George, I could never allow little Johnny to be tortured."

George: "I am sorry John, but according to your ideas of morality you must, for no matter how much torture Johnny suffers, he could not conceivably receive enough pain to outweigh all of the pleasure that $10,00.00 per person would create for 7 billion people, therefore, torturing little Johnny must be morally right."

John: "Perhaps I should rethink my moral decision making."

George: "Perhaps."

You may object here because the example is so silly, it is not reasonable to believe this kind of choice would be presented to little Johnny's father. While the example may be silly, it is silly on purpose. I am trying to show that simple calculations of pleasure and pain do not always help us make moral decisions. Little Johnny should not be tortured against his will, regardless of how much pleasure it may provide others. We know this instinctively. That is the Natural Law. It is those ideas of right and wrong that we instinctively know, and the other ideas of right and wrong that we can figure out from the things we know instinctively. For example, we know it is wrong to harm someone *physically* for selfish reasons. We know this instinctively. Because we know this rule, we can reason that it is wrong to harm someone *mentally* for selfish reasons. They are different kinds of harm, but because we know the first type of harm (physical harm) is wrong, we can see that it follows that the second type of harm (mental harm) is wrong as well.

The reason I am taking the time to make all of this clear is so you understand that when I stated that having a surgery to remove cancer is not a harm, I was not measuring the pleasure derived from a long life against the pain of having surgery. If that was what I meant, I would have stated that having a surgery is *less* of a harm than dying of cancer. What I actually stated was that having the surgery is *not* a harm at all. It is not a moral harm. This is *not* because of the relation between pleasures and pains, but because life is a higher good than having a pain-free body. 'Life is to be preserved,' is one of the things we know instinctively from the Natural Law. So when trying to define moral harm, we can reason that saving a life is not a harm in this situation, even though there is physical pain involved.

Harm and Nature

We will now look at the concept of harm and nature. Earlier we talked about injury and pain to the body as types of harm under certain circumstances. Consider again our cancer example. While we found that surgery was a good (even though it caused injury) because it saved a life, we would not consider the same injury caused by surgery to be a good if the person who was injured did not have cancer. This is because, generally, when someone is purposely injured, as in the case of surgery, there must be a higher good to *justify* the injury. What if there was no higher good? What if a doctor performed surgery on a person for no reason at all? That injury *would be* a moral harm. Injuring someone for no reason is certainly evil. But why is injuring someone evil? In order to answer this question we need to look at nature. When I use the word nature here I mean the way the world works. In other words, nature is what normally occurs if nothing interferes.

In the case of injury by unnecessary surgery, we must know what the human body would be like, in nature, without unnecessary surgery. Then we must contrast that with what happens when unnecessary surgery interferes with nature. In nature, assuming no disease or other malfunction, the human body should be whole, healthy, and pain-free. By doing unnecessary surgery we are compromising the state of nature by damaging the body, making it less healthy and more likely to contract disease. By cutting the body we are breaking up the natural state of the body. We are damaging skin and muscle, causing the body pain, and, depending on where we cut, taking away the natural function of a certain part of the body. If we cut the brain, or the eye, we may permanently destroy the function of that body part. To do this for no reason is unnatural. It causes harm to the individual and harm to nature, for it causes both pain to the individual and injury to nature (because your body is a part of nature).

Murder would cause the same problems for the same reasons. What I mean when I say a 'harm to nature' is that nature operates in a certain way and when nature is altered or destroyed for no good reason, a harm has been done to nature. I am not intending to make a person out of nature. Nature is 'the way things work.' It is the system that unites every human. It is the system that contains the elements of life for every human. When we harm nature, in some sense, we harm everyone, including ourselves. This is not to say that every alteration, or even destruction, of nature is a harm. As we learn how nature works we are sometimes able to alter nature so nature can thrive. We work *within* the rules of nature, for the *benefit* of nature. Far from being a harm to nature, this kind of alteration is good for nature. For example, cultivating land so you can grow organic crops to feed people is a good thing because, whether you hold a naturalistic/evolutionary view or a theistic/design view, people are the highest beings in nature and they should be preserved. Controlled burning in some forests may be a good thing, because, if it is not done, larger, more destructive fires will probably happen. There are many examples I could parade here, but I think it is sufficient to state that there are many alterations of nature that are positive. There are also alterations of nature that are negative. These negative alterations are harms to nature, a fact that many environmentalists have pointed out with great moral authority.

I take no position here on genetically modified foods, deforestation, and the manufacture of carbon emissions. However, I will say that such modifications, if they harm nature, must justify themselves by showing that some higher good is achieved because of them. My point is not to sidetrack you into other moral questions, but to show that there is such a thing as moral harm to nature. Harms to nature are ultimately harms to people, because people are in nature and we all use nature together. Your harm to nature by destroying a forest may be a harm to me because I will never get to experience that forest or see the animals who live there, or because the cure to some disease my child suffers from was lost in the destruction of that forest. If you destroy that forest without a good reason, you harm me and yourself, you harm your neighbor. The same is true if you damage your neighbor's eye. In that case you have not only damaged your neighbor specifically, but you may have damaged everyone else generally. Your neighbor may have been the person who was going to discover a cure for AIDS or paint the next masterpiece, but she is less likely to do so now because she has been harmed. We do not live in a vacuum. Harm to anyone, or anything for that matter, may be harm to everyone, or everything.

Unjustified harms to nature are unnatural. That is to say, unnatural acts are harms. They are evils. When the Natural Law says "do no harm" it means do no wrong, do no evil, do nothing against the natural order, *do nothing unnatural.*

'Party Based Morality'

One criticism of some Christians is that they scream and yell against abortion, homosexual sex, and Hollywood, but they do not seem to care about throwing their plastic bottles in the garbage can, treating animals badly in the name of convenience, or taking care of the poor and oppressed in society. At the same time some non-Christians are accused of whining and lecturing about the environment and the poor, while supporting abortion and sexual deviance in society. Whether or not these criticisms are true (and for most people they are not), they highlight an important issue we should analyze. There is no question that if we ought to do no harm in one area, we also ought to do no harm in any other. I believe the criticisms above occur because some people have adopted the views of political parties and other groups rather than thinking through moral issues for themselves. This 'party based morality' likely affects individuals from every political party, interest group, and subculture. 'It's right because that is the Republican way' or 'the Democrat way' or 'the Baptist way' or the 'Sierra Club way' or the 'Donny Osmond fan club way.' The reason I bring this up in this chapter is because, as we try to chase down the truth about the morality of homosexual sexual activity, we need to do so *without* unthinking loyalty to views adopted from political parties, interest groups, or subcultures. We must think for ourselves.

Now that we have our framework for understanding what it means to 'do no harm,' we can apply this knowledge in our attempt to discover whether homosexual sexual relationships are morally wrong.

CHAPTER 10

Love Can't Be Wrong

In the last chapter I did not write much about homosexual sex. The reason for that is because we were setting up a framework that will help us understand morality in general. We will now return to looking at Natural Law arguments made by those who are carrying the burden of proof to show that homosexual sexual activity is morally justified.

This chapter will deal with an argument that consists of one modest phrase: 'Love can't be wrong.' This argument, at first blush, seems obviously true. Taken outside any particular context, this statement is true and is at the very heart of the Natural Law. Love *is* right. Love is always right. But not all actions that claim to flow from love are loving actions.

I will begin with a few outrageous and obvious examples. Hitler's 'love' for the German people caused him to become convinced that it was morally right to massacre Jewish people. The KKK's 'love' for the white race caused them to become convinced that harming black people was morally right. A teenage boy's 'love' for his sweetheart causes him to steal the gift of her virginity from her future husband.

I could go on but I think we can all see that we will have to agree on a definition of love before we can allow the word to be used as a trump card to justify all manner of evil actions. We must analyze what the people who use the 'love can't be wrong' argument mean by 'love.'

We will start with what we know they mean. We know they mean romantic sexual love between two people of the same gender, because that is the particular act they are trying to justify. However, that definition does not help us since it would be the same thing as saying 'romantic sexual love between two people of the same gender can't be wrong.' And, while that may be the argument they advocate, it cannot be what they mean by the word 'love.' Because, that would not be an argument, but just a statement, that we already know they believe. Such a statement would do nothing to further the persuasiveness of their moral argument.

It is possible that they mean romantic love generally, the kind of love between two people that causes them to want to be together and to form a sexual union with one another as an expression of their love. However, I do not believe this could be what they mean either, since I assume most of them would find the love between a 60 year old man and a 14 year old girl, or even worse, the love between a brother and a sister, repugnant and morally wrong. However, no one can deny that both the 60 year old man and the 14 year old girl, and the brother and sister, could be romantically in 'love' with one another.

I do not know if they know what they mean. They may be doing nothing more than appealing to the emotions of the people they are trying to convince. However, if they mean anything, they must mean love in the selfless sense. They must mean love in the sense that one person wants the best for another person. True love: the selfless, sacrificial, feelings and actions which desire to be with the beloved, but more importantly, desire to seek the best and highest things for the beloved. If that is the sense in which they use the word Love (and it is the only sense in which the argument would have any chance of persuading anyone), then we must know more about homosexual sexual activity to know whether it could really be an expression of True love.

If homosexual sex is an expression of True love, then it is certainly morally right. If homosexual sex is not an expression of True love, that does not necessarily prove that homosexual sexual activity is morally wrong, but it would show that the 'love can't be wrong' argument is useless as a moral justification of homosexual sex.

Sex

Let us begin by analyzing sexual activity itself. I must warn the reader that **what follows is not intended for children.**

At its climax, sex is generally marked by strong physical sensations in the genitalia. This does not exclude the possibility that one can engage in sexual activity without a climax being reached. However the generally accepted end for sexual activity is a physical climax. The most common method for achieving that climax in heterosexual sexual relations involves the joining of genitalia in male female intercourse. It requires no great imagination to see that the genitalia of the male and the female are particularly suited for this activity; I would even argue that the male and female physical bodies appear to be obviously designed with this activity in mind. This is proven not just by the shape and function of the body parts, but by the fact that no one reasonably suggests that anything less than the overwhelming majority of human beings throughout all time have enjoyed sex in a male-female context. Male-female sex is obviously a natural union. This is born out even further by the fact that it is through this type of union and only through this type of union (or a copy of this type of union), that children are conceived. Since the begetting of children is as natural as any physical activity known, the evidence is squarely in favor of the proposition that male-female sexual activity is a natural and normal event.

The above, of course, says nothing one way or the other about whether or not homosexual sexual activity is natural or normal, however it does give us a framework from which to judge the activity. Still, before we move on to homosexual sexual activity I think we must clarify the *context* in which male-female sexual activity is normal or natural. We have established that heterosexual sex is natural and normal generally, but the context in which it takes place must pass the same test.

As we know, sex between men and women happens in many contexts. Rape, for instance, will often lead to sexual climax for one person and certainly can result in the begetting of a child. This is the same for incest, pedophilia, adultery and fornication.[1] When we analyze the thread woven through each of these activities, one thing becomes apparent: these activities are morally harmful to both people involved.

In the case of rape, the harm is easy to see. The person who is being forced into sex is obviously harmed, both physically and in the sense that they are being dehumanized. The rapist is being harmed by the fact that he is engaging in immoral behavior, the fact that he is likely to be punished by society, and the fact

---

[1] Fornication – sexual relations between people who are not married

that he will likely suffer from the guilt and shame connected with victimizing and dehumanizing another human being. Any child of this type of union is being harmed by the fact that he will not have a mother and father who are raising him together, or worse, he may be murdered in the womb before he gets a chance at life at all because of the burden or shame that his mother feels. Society at large is harmed by the fear created by these kinds of violent acts, and society is burdened with the enormous cost of trial and punishment of the criminal. The ripple effect of such harms is substantial.

Pedophilia (I am here discussing the crime in a male-female context although other contexts are all too common) causes harm to the child who is taken advantage of, in most cases by an adult in a position of trust. The child is harmed physically, often by the activity itself, and emotionally in more ways than I have room to describe here. Again, the victim of this crime is dehumanized. If a child is begotten through this crime, the child has the same harms to look forward to as the child in the case of rape, including the possibility that the criminal will force the mother to murder the child through abortion in order to cover his crime. The pedophile himself is harmed in all of the same ways as the rapist.

In the case of incest (let us assume in a non-pedophile, consensual context), the people are both harmed by the fact that they have committed an unnatural and shameful act. They have perverted the nature of the family bonds they share. They will suffer guilt and emotional scarring. Any child who is begotten will possibly suffer from more than the child of rape or pedophilia in that there is a higher probability that the child born under such circumstances will be born with physical abnormalities. Those abnormalities will increase the difficulties he will face his whole life. The child will most likely also suffer from the stigma and shame associated with having parents who are close relatives. A child in this situation also may lose his life through abortion because of the shame of his parents.

Now we get to the two instances that are not illegal, but are no less immoral.

Adultery harms more than just the people involved in the sexual activity. In order to commit adultery there must be at least one third party: the spouse of one of the adulterers. This person is harmed by having his trust destroyed, his relationship with his spouse damaged, and the emotional pain caused by rejection, because the adulterer chose to engage in such an intimate activity with a person outside the marriage. Adultery also harms both of the adulterers because they have engaged in an unnatural and shameful activity. They have perverted the sanctity of marriage. They will share the guilt and emotional scarring that follows from taking part in an act that was so harmful to another human being. Adultery harms any child of the marriage that has been violated, especially if the adultery leads to a divorce. It also harms any child that results from the affair, because the child is not likely to be raised by his biological parents. This child may also be murdered in the womb to cover the adulterers' immoral actions.

The last context we will analyze where sexual relationships are harmful is fornication. One harm caused by fornication is the fact that each person involved is taking liberties with the other person's body that are not matched by the level of commitment that has been given. The proper level of commitment for a sexual relationship is a lifelong monogamous marriage commitment. This level of commitment is important. It is built into human beings because of the emotional well-being it produces. When people engage in sexual activity without this level of commitment, emotional suffering follows. This is also why the divorce of a marriage relationship is so harmful. Sexual activity outside of marriage also shows an improper commitment to any possible child who may be born from the sexual union. A child is best cared for by a loving mother and father who are married and committed to each other for life. Outside this type of committed relationship, the child does not have the same chance at a healthy life.

Fornication causes other types of harm as well, including the spreading to another person of a sexually transmitted disease. As we all know, if all sexual relationships only happened within a committed, monogamous marriage, then sexually transmitted diseases would generally not exist. Sexually transmitted diseases exist and thrive *because* people engage in the types of sexual behavior described above.

There is another issue at play with fornication, the issue of consent. At this point the reader may ask whether a lesser commitment than marriage may be appropriate since those engaging in the sexual activity consent to the activity without a marriage commitment. The problem with such consent, beyond what has been described above, is that all of the parties necessary to give their consent to such a relationship are not able to consent. For instance, the future spouses of the people involved in the sexual activity may not be inclined to give their consent for their future spouse to engage in sexual activity with another person. This may lead to regret and shame for those who take part in fornication because they have deprived their future spouse of the gift of their virginity. Even presuming the future spouse would give her consent, any child which may result from the sexual activity cannot consent, and the child, according to the Natural Law, is entitled to a mother and father who are married and committed to one another for life.

When a person intentionally engages in sexual relationships outside of marriage, he is always treating his sexual partner as a *thing,* as an *object* to be used for his own personal pleasure. If he truly desired the best for the other person, he would not put the cart before the horse. He would make sure that he had *given* the level of commitment that is proper to a sexual relationship before he *took* the other person's body in sexual activity. We can all see how much damage fornication and a general lack of commitment has caused by the high number of fatherless homes in this world, and the resulting harm often suffered by the children in these homes.

Homosexual Sexual Activity

We have now come to the place in this book where we deal directly with homosexual sexual activity. In the last section, I talked about marriage and its role providing the framework for a lifelong, committed, monogamous relationship, where sexual activity was truly safe and edifying, because the necessary level of commitment was present to satisfy both the physical and emotional results of that sexual activity.

History has shown us that marriage between a man and a woman is the best framework for raising families and supporting the physical and emotional needs of the spouses. The problem is, that to be fair to homosexual "marriage" proponents, a historical argument, by itself, does not solve the problem, because homosexual "marriage" has almost no history.

Homosexual "marriage" has only existed for a few years in very, very few places. However, I do believe, historically speaking, marriage between a man and a woman, at its best, is clearly a good thing. I am referring to a marriage between a man and a woman at its best, just as when discussing homosexual "marriage" I will refer to it at its best. To view either at their worst would do nothing to promote an understanding of the issues. One side would say 'look at such and such negative thing that exists in some homosexual "marriages."'

The person responding would say: 'But look at such and such a negative thing that exists in some heterosexual marriages.'

In order to have a discussion about whether homosexual "marriage" is moral, the advocate for homosexual "marriage" only needs to show that it could be moral at its best. The fact that some people, or even many people, will have bad homosexual "marriages" does not show that homosexual "marriage" is morally wrong. The bad marriages are an issue of context. Sometimes people will make wrong choices and harm relationships. This does not show that the type of relationship is wrong; it only shows that an individual or individuals have harmed the relationship through bad choices. For example, there are many bad mothers who harm their relationships with their children, and many bad children who harm their relationships with their mothers. However, no reasonable person would suggest that relationships between mothers and their children, in general, are morally wrong because of this.

This goes both ways. The argument is equally ineffective when used against the proponent of homosexual "marriage" and when used as a proof by the advocate of homosexual "marriage" that 'heterosexual marriage is not working either.' We must dismiss such arguments and analyze the question of whether homosexual "marriages" can possibly be morally right, not whether every homosexual "marriage" or heterosexual marriage will, in fact, work out perfectly.

Children

The statistics on fatherless or motherless homes hardly need to be displayed here for the reader to agree that a home with a mother and a father, who are married and committed to one another for life, is an ideal arrangement for the raising of children. This brings up at least two fair questions:

1. Do homosexual "marriages" also provide an ideal arrangement for the raising of children?

2. What about homosexual "marriages" where there will be no children?

In order to fully answer the first question, we must consider the answer to the ultimate question posed by this book: is homosexual sexual activity morally wrong? If we find that homosexual sexual activity is morally wrong, then the family arrangement in a homosexual "marriage" includes a lifestyle, for the parents, based upon an immoral activity. The promotion of an immoral lifestyle does not provide an ideal environment for the raising of children. However, even if we were to conclude that homosexual sexual activity was not morally wrong, it would not necessarily follow that homosexual "marriages" provided an ideal family arrangement for the raising of children. This gives us a place to begin the analysis without having to answer the ultimate question posed by this book yet.

Children need parents to care for their emotional and physical needs. It is equally clear from our experience that some parents are better than others. For instance, mothers who are manipulative and withholding are not going to raise physically and emotionally well-adjusted children as well as mothers who are honest and unconditionally loving. Fathers who are harsh and physically abusive are not going to raise physically and emotionally well-adjusted children as well as fathers who are kind and exercise proper discipline techniques. The real question is whether the *gender* of mothers and fathers is important, assuming that the parents are parenting well.

There are distinct differences between the genders. The most obvious differences are physical. Men and women have different bodies. Men and women also tend to be different psychologically and emotionally. Notice that I used the word 'tend' in the last sentence but not the sentence before it. The second sentence refers to a tendency in people and not necessarily an absolute difference in every case. As where every physically normal man and woman have major differences in their bodies, not every man and woman appear to have major differences emotionally and psychologically. Some men seem to take actions and have feelings we would normally expect from women. The same can be said for some women who seem to take actions and have feelings we would normally expect from men. In our experience, we can probably agree that these types of men and women are rare, at least in the case of men and women who exhibit these actions and feelings in a major way; for example, a man who exhibits actions and feelings that appear to be *completely* like what we would expect from a woman.

Is a child being raised in the ideal environment when he is raised by a man and a woman who exhibit the actions and feelings that are natural for a man and a woman? The research suggests that two parents are better than one, and further that mothers and fathers each perform an important role in the raising of physically and emotionally well-adjusted children. We cannot reasonably assume that this is due *solely* to the differences in the physical bodies of the man and woman who are the child's parents. It must, at least to some extent, be due to the psychological and emotional differences in men and women. The question then becomes: Can two men or two women provide an environment for a child that is just as good as the environment a man and a woman provide?

Earlier I noted that some men and some women appear to exhibit actions and feelings we would normally associate with the opposite gender. If it was the case that all homosexual "marriages" were made up of one person who exhibited actions and feelings that completely correspond to his own gender and one person who exhibited actions and feelings that completely corresponded to the other gender, perhaps an argument could be made that a child could be provided with the emotional and physical nurturing needed to become well-adjusted. However, I do not know of anyone who would make such a claim. In fact, a strong argument can be made that a person who exhibits actions and feelings associated with a different gender than his own, is not well-adjusted himself, as evidenced by the fact that he does not act and feel in the way he *naturally* ought to act and feel.

I can imagine the objections that are rising at this point in the minds of some of you, but I humbly ask that you put this book down and take five minutes to honestly consider whether men and women are naturally different and whether those differences are good and important.

If some of you decide there are no differences between men and women, then my reply is that you either have very little experience getting to know people from both genders, or you are simply being dishonest with yourself because you have decided such differences do not fit in with the worldview you have adopted. If the latter is the case, I recommend you consider the consequences of continuing to hold a worldview that is so clearly inconsistent with facts that are so obvious. These facts are, and have historically been, almost universally accepted. If some of you have decided that the differences between men and women are unimportant, I would simply encourage you to embrace the wonder of your gender. Women are amazing, complicated, and special human beings, gifted with qualities that are unique to their gender. Men, are equally amazing, and are endowed with very special and important qualities that are unique to their gender.

An important question to consider is whether
two people who are unable to naturally produce a
child are likely to be the best group to raise a child.
This is not the time for emotional arguments. I am
asking you to consider this question seriously. Human
beings are complicated, and they seem to benefit from
the input of two opposite gendered parents. This
makes sense, because only two opposite gendered
parents are physically capable of conceiving a child. If
we are considering whether parents of the same
gender are equally fit to raise children, we must offer
some reason why the difference in gender is not
important, or we must offer some reason why, even
though having two parents of opposite gender is good
and natural, having two parents of the same gender is
equally good or better. Some people claim there are
many children without parents who would benefit
from being adopted by two parents of the same gender
more than they would benefit from living with no
parents at all. This argument does not solve the
problem. Even if the argument was true, it would only
apply to a relatively small number of children who are
not able to find a home with male and female parents.
The argument would not provide any justification for

same gendered parents who have a child with a sperm donor or surrogate parent, or for same gendered parents who adopt children who could also have been adopted by a married man and woman.

Please take note that I am not attempting to prove any conclusion about the relative *ability* of any *individual* same gendered parent to raise children. I am simply bringing up some ideas to consider. There is no way that I know of to prove the effectiveness of any particular set of parents with hard science. However, I do believe we can all objectively ask ourselves some of the questions posed above and honestly conclude that it is most likely the best situation for a child to be raised by the child's biological parents, or adoptive, opposite gender married parents, in a loving and committed home.

The second question posed above was: What about homosexual "marriages" without children? There is a preliminary problem with this question. Very few individuals, if any, are advocating for the legalization of homosexual "marriage" in a context where children would not be allowed to be raised by the individuals in the "marriage." Nevertheless, in order to fully explore the merits of homosexual "marriage" we need to look at homosexual "marriage" relationships outside the context of raising children, since there will likely be many people who will enter into a homosexual "marriage" without any intention of raising children.

To answer this question we must finally tackle the question of whether homosexual sexual relationships are natural and morally right. It is true that even if a homosexual sexual relationship is natural and morally right, it does not necessarily follow that homosexual "marriage" is natural and morally right. However, it would be strong evidence that some recognition of such relationships would be morally right.

Earlier we discussed perversions of sexual relationships as well as natural sexual relationships between married men and women. Sex has consequences. The consequences of sexual activity are both physical and emotional. Some of the physical consequences of sex can be pregnancy and sound health, as well as disease and decreased health. Some of the emotional consequences of sexual activity can be joy, emotional fulfillment and increased feelings of well-being, as well as depression, shame, guilt, anger, and feelings of being used.

It is obvious, to everyone who is honest, that male and female bodies are designed for sexual intercourse between opposite genders. The sexual organs literally fit together naturally and even naturally prepare for sexual activity through erection and lubrication.

As I wrote earlier, even within the context of male female sexual activity, there are perversions (rape, incest, fornication, adultery). However there is a context where none of the negative physical and emotional consequences of sexual activity necessarily exist. Notice I did not state that the negative consequences never exist. I said they do not *necessarily* exist. If a man and a woman abstain from sexual activity until they have entered a lifelong monogamous commitment to one another in marriage, disease is extremely unlikely to result. Shame, guilt, anger, and feelings of being used are also unlikely to result, and a pregnancy is far less likely to result in a single parent raising a child. In fact, physical and emotional well-being are most likely to occur in a relationship of this type.

The question is: 'Does homosexual sexual activity *necessarily* have negative consequences?' Once again the ultimate question is at play in any complete answer, because, if homosexual sex is morally wrong, then the fact that it is wrong is a negative consequence in itself. In other words, those who participate in homosexual sex would be harming themselves and each other *because* they are taking part in an activity that is morally wrong.

First, we will simply look at some of the same negative consequences we outlined above. In male-male homosexual sex, there are negative physical consequences that result from the activity itself. It is not my intention to outline all of the medical science related to male-male sexual activity. A simple Google™ search will turn up all the evidence needed to convince any honest reader that sexual activity between males, even in the most controlled environment (monogamy, use of prophylactics etc.), is unhealthy. That is not to say that heterosexual sexual activity is always healthy either. There are male-female partners who engage in forms of sexual activity that are unnatural and physically dangerous. However, normal male-female intercourse, in a monogamous marriage relationship, does not carry the dangers that male-male sexual activity does.

Consider what Dr. John Diggs wrote in *The Health Risks of Gay Sex*:

Anal intercourse is the sine qua non of sex for many gay men. Yet human physiology makes it clear that the body was not designed to accommodate this activity. The rectum is significantly different from the vagina with regard to suitability for penetration by a penis. The vagina has natural lubricants and is supported by a network of muscles. It is composed of a mucus membrane with a multi-layer stratified squamous epithelium that allows it to endure friction without damage and to resist the immunological actions caused by semen and sperm. In comparison, the anus is a delicate mechanism of small muscles that comprise an "exit-only" passage. With repeated trauma, friction and stretching, the sphincter loses its tone and its ability to maintain a tight seal. Consequently, anal intercourse leads to leakage of fecal material that can easily become chronic.

The potential for injury is exacerbated by the fact that the intestine has only a single layer of cells separating it from highly vascular tissue, that is, blood. Therefore, any organisms that are introduced into the rectum have a much easier time establishing a foothold for infection than they would in a vagina. The single layer tissue cannot withstand the friction associated with penile penetration, resulting in traumas that expose both participants to blood, organisms in feces, and a mixing of bodily fluids.

Furthermore, ejaculate has components that are immunosuppressive. In the course of ordinary reproductive physiology, this allows the sperm to evade the immune defenses of the female. Rectal insemination of rabbits has shown that sperm impaired the immune defenses of the recipient. Semen may have a similar impact on humans.

The end result is that the fragility of the anus and rectum, along with the immunosuppressive effect of ejaculate, make anal-genital intercourse a most efficient manner of transmitting HIV and other infections. The list of diseases found with extraordinary frequency among male homosexual practitioners as a result of anal intercourse is alarming[.][2]

I am not arguing that all men who engage in homosexual sexual activity do so through anal sex. However, it is certainly not uncommon. Anal sex is obviously harmful, even when engaged in by monogamous partners.

Female-female sexual activity is admittedly not as physically dangerous as male-male sexual activity. However, there is research that suggests there are dangers involved. One real and serious danger related to female-female sexual activity and male-male sexual

---

[2] Diggs, John R. Jr.; *The Health Risks of Gay Sex.* p. 3 (Corporate R esource Council, 2002) Retrieved from http://catholiceducation.or g/articles/homosexuality/healthrisksSSA.pdf; last visited June 15, 2 013.

activity is beyond the simply physical. The research shows that those who engage in homosexual sexual activity are far more likely to suffer from mental disease.

A variety of psychological disorders present themselves at high rates among those who practice homosexual sex. Some make the argument that the prevalence of these conditions is due to the lack of acceptance in society of the lifestyle of those who engage in homosexual sex. However, this argument is losing credibility as the rates of these psychological issues continue to be high even in places where homosexual sex, and those who practice it, are widely accepted by society. If the prevalence of these mental conditions was related to acceptance, one would expect to see the level of psychological disorders closely related to the level of acceptance of homosexual sexual activity in the society. Because that correlation is not apparent, there must be some other reason why these conditions are so widespread.

Unnatural

Take a moment and remove yourself, or your loved one, or your neighbor from the equation.

Remove all emotion and all references in your mind to those who have been ill-treated by people who advocate against homosexual sex. Just look at the Natural Law. Homosexual sexual activity is obviously unnatural. In other words, an objective person, without any agenda, could literally look at the human body and be shown heterosexual sexual relations and homosexual sexual relations. Without a moment's hesitation he would identify heterosexual sexual activity as a natural human activity, and homosexual sexual activity as an unnatural human activity. This is simple round peg, square hole logic. There is no reasonable argument to suggest that homosexual sex is a natural behavior when the physical activity is analyzed outside the context of the feelings of the individuals involved. In other words, if a particular woman did not sexually desire another particular woman, there would be no question that, from a natural, physical perspective, they were not a match sexually. Read what a nurse had to say in an article on this subject:

I am a nurse so I understand why homosexuality is wrong anatomically.

There is no anatomic union between a man and a man or a woman and a woman. There are no parts that healthily fit in either sexual union. A woman and a woman do not fit together. In the sexual act, they stay outside of any union or find devices to simulate the natural sexual act between a man and a woman. A man and a man do the same thing. They simulate the union of man and women [*sic*] by having a sexual act in an area of the body that is very unclean, the colon. Both lesbians and homosexual men are artificially copying the natural sexual union of a man and a woman.[3]

At the beginning of this book I included the story of The Emperor's New Clothes. Imagine the little boy in that story being introduced to the concept of heterosexual and homosexual sex. He would blurt out what was obvious to everyone who is honest.

[3] From the Concerned Women for America website: http://www.c wfa.org/articledisplay.asp?id=20761&department=FIELD&categor yid=misc. Last visited May 25, 2013.

"Homosexual sex doesn't make sense." This is obvious and true. If not for the pressure put on people to accept this behavior, everyone else would say the same thing. Ask yourself these questions: If a man was supposed to have sex with other men, why would he be born with a body obviously designed to have sex with a woman? Why would he be given a body capable of producing children through heterosexual sex? The same questions apply to homosexual women. Homosexual sexual activity is clearly a perversion. It goes against the clear design of the human body.

Some who want to justify homosexual sexual activity realize this and answer this argument by saying that evolution has made some people homosexual for the purpose of population control. This argument fails to understand the theory of evolution. Even if one accepts the evolutionary theory, it is clear that naturalistic evolution does not *make* anything. Evolution has no mind. Evolution is a theoretical description of a process where genetic mutations that are beneficial to a species tend to thrive, and mutations that are not beneficial tend to decrease. Homosexual sexual activity does not tend to increase the population (because homosexuals do not reproduce through a homosexual sexual union), nor does homosexual sex increase health, as the medical literature shows. Therefore, if homosexual desires are genetic (which is unproven), that fact would defy the theory of evolution. Again, this argument, which attempts to define the unnatural as natural, does not work.

When we as a society proclaim that homosexual sexual activity is morally justified, we encourage those with homosexual attractions to engage in homosexual sexual activity, rather than encouraging them to attempt to develop attractions toward the opposite sex. This deprives our world of the intelligent, talented, beautiful, and wonderful children these people might produce if they were in heterosexual marriages.

Earlier I showed that the concept of the unnatural and the concept of harm are the same. That which is unnatural is harmful and that which is harmful is wrong. Those things that people have created that do not exist in the natural world must harness the natural world or enhance the natural world in order to be useful and good. At its base, the fact that homosexual sexual activity is unnatural and harmful, is why homosexual sex is morally wrong.

Again I ask you to remember the story of the Emperor and his new clothes. We now live in a society where being loud and aggressive and, even more so, being 'cool,' is all it takes to silence the people. For those readers old enough to remember (and you do not need to be very old), homosexuality used to be widely considered to be a perversion in our society. I am not talking about 200 years ago; I am talking about 20 to 30 years ago. Of course, there are many places in our society where this is still the case. Furthermore, like the people in the story, I think many who remain silent still understand the Natural Law well enough to recognize that homosexual sexual activity is morally wrong. But the naked emperor parades in the streets and we are told that his clothes are beautiful and if we cannot see them we are idiots, bigots, hateful, and 'on the wrong side of history.' These are strong words. They make many people think twice before offering what they know to be the truth for fear of the social consequences.

Let me make this very clear. You are not doing anyone a favor by being silent, or by 'going with the

flow,' or by 'picking your battles.' You are harming the
emperor who would be better off putting on some
clothes so as not to freeze to death when the natural
world catches up with his nakedness. You are not
helping those around you by pretending to believe a lie
and encouraging them, by your silence, to believe the
lie themselves. You are not helping yourself either, by
being dishonest with yourself and not standing up for
the truth, whether it is popular to do so or not. There
has always been a battle for the morality of society;
and there always will be. Do not be like the people in
that story. Speak up for what is right, no matter how
others may treat you. But speak in love. Respect people.
Show people that the reason you speak is not to
condemn and to shame others, but to help others and
to show love. It is the friend helping the friend out of
the way of the oncoming bus. Be that friend, do not be
the bus.

If sexual activity is intended to be an
expression of love, then sexual activity that is morally
right needs to be a loving action. A loving action
cannot knowingly harm the beloved. As seen above,
male-male and female-female sexual activity is
unnatural and therefore harmful to the person who

engages in it. Because of this fact, neither person involved in male-male or female-female sexual activity can be loving the other person while engaging in that activity, because he or she knows the activity is harmful to the other person. This is true for any harmful sexual activity between any people, whether male-female, male-male, or female-female. This lack of love can and does occur in all of these contexts. The question above was whether this lack of love *necessarily* occurs within homosexual sexual activity. The answer is yes.

Because homosexual sexual activity is obviously unnatural, it is *only* when emotions are introduced that most people will even consider a possible moral justification for the activity. So the question we have asked is whether, even though the activity is obviously unnatural in itself, homosexual sexual activity might be justified on some other ground? The most common ground suggested, the ground that appeals to us as human beings most strongly, has been that those who want to engage in homosexual sexual activity want to do so because they love each other *and* they desire to act out that love through sex and "marriage." No reasonable person who is interested in what is morally right has respect for any sexual activity done in the context of pure lust. The dangers of that kind of sexual activity to a person's body and soul are obvious and well documented. But when our children, our siblings, our friends and our neighbors who we love and who we desire to see happy, come to us and tell us they cannot be happy in a heterosexual relationship, but they can be happy in a homosexual relationship, we naturally hurt for them. I also hurt for them.

My heart aches for the love that homosexual people desire. I want to see them be truly fulfilled in love. Love, after all, cannot be wrong. But, we have seen that homosexual sexual activity is not a loving activity. Engaging with your beloved in a physically unnatural (and therefore harmful) activity that may be physically dangerous, and often leads to psychological problems, is not loving. It is *not* loving.

This does not mean that those who engage in homosexual sexual activity do not love each other; far from it. These people often carry a deep love for one another. I am simply saying that love, in this context, is not truly *expressed* through sexual activity. A person can have a relationship with deep enduring love that does not involve sexual activity. Just think about your relationship with your mother or your father, your sister or your brother, your children, your friend, or your God. All of these relationships, at their best, are based on unconditional love. That love is expressed in many ways, none of which are sexual. A person can have an amazing relationship without sex. It is my belief, and the Natural Law persuades me I am correct, that in any relationship outside of a monogamous, loving marriage between a man and a woman, sexual activity deteriorates relationships; it does not build them up.

You may object at this point. I wrote in Chapter Nine that unnatural activities are harmful when they are *unjustified.* You may believe that emotional attraction to a behavior justifies the behavior. No behavior can justify itself solely on the basis of a corresponding attraction. When the day is done, every behavior we desire to engage in must justify itself by something other than our emotions. If we reject this idea, we are left with no standard to judge any behavior. We must be willing to subject the 'I want' to the 'I ought.' Doing what is morally right must have a higher priority in our lives than doing what we desire to do.

For the believer in Jesus Christ, we look forward to a time when this fallen world will end and all will be made right because of the amazing sacrifice made for all of our sins on the cross and the resurrection from the dead of our Savior, defeating death and hell. We all have to suppress some of our desires here on earth, recognizing that they have been twisted by a fallen world. When we get to the end and are face to face with God, we will suppress nothing, for nothing will be twisted any longer.

CHAPTER 11

<u>This is Who I Am</u>

Consider the following conversation:

George: "Georgette, you know that I love you and I want what is best for you. However you also know that I believe engaging in a homosexual sexual relationship is morally wrong."

Georgette: "George, you say that you love me, but you don't fully love me because you don't accept the fact that I am gay. Being gay is *who I am*. In order

to love me fully, you have to accept my
lifestyle, because it is *who I am.*"

Painful. For anyone who is in the place of
George or Georgette in this situation, there is going to
be pain. Georgette is going to feel pain because she
feels like George does not fully love her. She feels like
her homosexual lifestyle is part of her essence, part of
who she *is.* George is going to feel hurt because he
feels like he cannot be in a full relationship with
Georgette, he believes engaging in a homosexual
sexual relationship is morally wrong, and he knows
his belief causes conflict between him and Georgette.

Two questions become apparent to me:

1. Is being a homosexual part of who someone
   is?
2. Can someone love another person fully, but
   not accept the person's lifestyle?

First, understanding the concept of someone's
essence is difficult. However, I think we can discover
at least some part of what it means for something to be

part of who someone *is*. We can describe a person in many ways. Think about the following statements:

David is a lawyer.
David is a mediocre softball player.
David is a churchgoer.

These are things that David *does*. They could just as easily be put in the following manner:

David practices law.
David plays softball with average skill.
David attends church.

Think about these next statements:

David has two arms and two legs.
David has two children.
David has hazel eyes.

These are statements listing physical facts about David. They are things about David that can be easily observed. We will analyze one more set of sentences that describe David:

David is mean.

David is kind.

David is a heterosexual.

These statements seem to refer to more essential characteristics of David. The problem is that the first two statements contradict each other. If David has ever been mean to someone, then David is mean at least some of the time. The same is true for David's kindness. So actually, these sentences really just describe what David does. Like the first set of sentences, these statements describe actions. The question is whether this holds true, not just for David being mean and David being kind (as in the first two sentences), but also for David being heterosexual in the third sentence.

Is the third sentence somehow different than the first two? When people say that being homosexual is part of who they *are*, they must answer this question 'yes.' So what do they mean? First we need to figure out what they cannot mean. They cannot mean that the act of having sex with someone of their own gender is who they *are*, because that would only describe a particular behavior. They would only be describing what they do, which is the same thing being done in the first two sentences. If they happened to engage in heterosexual sex for some reason, they would not consider themselves to have changed who they *are* in their essence. Perhaps George and John can make this clear for us:

> **George:** "Being a kind and patient man is who I *am.*"
>
> **John:** "What are you talking about George? I remember a time when you were quite impatient and mean to me."
>
> **George:** "I do not deny that John, but that was a long time ago. Nowadays I am quite patient and kind."
>
> **John:** "Perhaps that is so, however, if you have been impatient and mean, then you are impatient and mean at least some of the time."
>
> **George:** "I see your point, and you're quite right, I have acted that way in the past. It is even possible that I may act that way in the future. But what I am trying to tell you is

that being kind and patient is who I *am*. It is what I desire to be in the deepest part of myself."

I think George's last statement is, and must be, what the homosexual means when she says being a homosexual is part of who she *is*. She must be describing a *feeling* that she considers to be an *essential* part of who she *is*. This feeling must be a personal feeling. In other words, it is not a thing that others can observe for themselves. George and John will explain:

George: "Face it like a man John, you are a criminal, it's just who you *are*."

John: "You are right that I am a criminal. I have committed many crimes, but that is not who I *am*. I could stop committing crimes today. The only reason I commit crimes is because I want things I cannot afford. Being a criminal is not essential to who I *am*. If I had enough money to buy what I wanted I would never commit another crime."

George: "But all *I see* is you committing crimes."

John: "George, you can't see what's inside me. Being a criminal is certainly not who I am."

George can only guess at what John is, in his essence, by what John does. George cannot know what is inside John. He cannot see John's thoughts and feelings. John is correct. He could stop committing crimes today. If we base a person's essence on his thoughts and feelings, then if John really *is* a criminal, that would be true even if he never committed any crimes; and, if John really *is not* a criminal, that would be true no matter how many crimes he committed.

These thoughts and feelings are important and they certainly are part of what makes us who we are. The question is, do we have a choice about which thoughts and feelings we choose to include in our personal identity?

I may have strong feelings and desires to be a great father to my children. I may desire this intensely. I may also desire to watch a movie, or play cards with my friends, or stay at work, on the same evening that my son has a baseball game. I may choose to do one of these other things rather than be there for my son. Which of these desires is who I *am*? Is it the desire to be a great father or the desire to play cards? If asked, I can choose to identify myself with either of these desires. Of course, my son may disagree with the way I identify myself, especially if I always choose to play cards rather than attend his sporting events. For the reader who has come to this book with an open mind and a desire to discover what is morally right, I will guess that one of the things you would identify as part of who you *are* is that you are a moral person. You are a person who desires to do what is morally right. You would identify yourself with that desire. You would agree that being a moral person is part of who you *are*.

This leaves us in the same place we have been for most of this book. We must know whether homosexual sex is morally right or morally wrong in order to know whether anyone should want to *identify* as a homosexual. We have seen that the homosexual lifestyle is clearly not what a person is referring to when he says being a homosexual is part of who he *is*. This is because a lifestyle is what a person does; it is the total of a person's actions. We have seen that the homosexual cannot be referring to those actions, but rather he must be referring to personal thoughts and feelings.

The question then is, must a person *necessarily* identify himself as a homosexual? Must he claim that being a homosexual is part of who he *is?* Before we answer that question we must answer the second question I asked earlier: can someone love a person fully and not accept the person's lifestyle?

The answer to this second question is: it depends. It depends on whether the lifestyle in question is moral or immoral. If your child was a drug addict and a murderer, could you still love him fully even though you do not accept his lifestyle? Of course you could. Your love for your child is unconditional; it is not based on your child's actions. If your child is a drug addict and a murderer, he is doing things that are morally wrong and therefore harmful to him and others. Not only can you love your child and reject his lifestyle, but you *ought* to love him and you *ought* to reject his lifestyle. To *accept* a lifestyle that harms your child is not loving.

At the same time, if your child is exercising regularly, eating right, and giving aid to the poor and oppressed, and you reject that lifestyle, you would not be fully loving your child. This is because your child's lifestyle is morally right and your child is doing something morally positive both for herself and for others. To reject *that* lifestyle is not loving, because you would not be desiring what is best for your child. In each case, accepting or rejecting your child's actions is loving if the acceptance or rejection is based on a desire for what is best for your child.

Earlier I wrote a fictional conversation between George and Georgette. One of the things Georgette said was "...In order to love me, you have to accept my lifestyle...." As we have seen, this is true only if Cara's lifestyle is morally right. If her lifestyle is morally wrong, then she must be harming herself. Therefore, for George to accept her lifestyle would not be loving, because it would not be desiring what is best for her.

Now we can analyze the other questions I posed which were: Must a person *necessarily* identify himself as a homosexual? *Must* he claim that being a homosexual is part of who he *is?* When I write 'being a homosexual,' I mean having personal thoughts and feelings of attraction for people of one's own gender. Thoughts and feelings are as much a part of a person as his leg. In other words, they are as much a part of a person as any physical characteristic. But, they are no *more* a part of a person than any other thoughts and feelings he has. All of our thoughts and feelings make up who we are. My desire to be a great father and my desire to play cards are both part of who I am as much as any physical part of my body. However, I can choose which of these thoughts and feelings I want to *identify* as who I *am*.

I sometimes have a strong desire to lie in order to cover up some wrong thing I have done. However, I do not choose to identify myself as a liar. In fact, I try not to lie because I have other thoughts and feelings that make me want to do what is morally right. People who have homosexual thoughts and feelings are not homosexuals in their *essence*, it is not who they *are* in any sense that necessarily *must* make up their identity any more than being a liar necessarily *must* make up my identity.

My right leg is part of who I am, but if I was constantly using it to kick cute little cats and children I may be better off cutting it off, or at least disabling it. The fact that you may have homosexual thoughts and desires does not mean that you must identify yourself as a homosexual. Even less does it mean that you must engage in homosexual sex. If homosexuality is unnatural, harmful, and therefore morally wrong, you should work to battle against those thoughts and feelings just as much as you should battle against any other thoughts and feelings that make you want to do immoral things.

Please pay attention here. There is *nothing* morally wrong about having thoughts and feelings that make you want to do what is unnatural and immoral. I myself, and all other people, have thoughts and feelings that make us want to do what is unnatural and immoral. If you have homosexual thoughts and feelings, let go of any shame. For those of you who do not have homosexual thoughts and feelings, STOP trying to shame those who do. You are not any better than the person who has these thoughts and feelings. You would not want everyone else shaming you for your immoral personal thoughts and feelings.

We are free. You are free to make choices. You can let your thoughts and feelings *define* you, or you can let your actions *define* you. Once again, the words of Dr. Martin Luther King ring out in truth: we should not judge by the color of a person's skin (or any other physical quality, or any other thoughts or feelings a person has), but by the content of her character [1]

For those who are wondering what you ought to do when you suffer with such strong thoughts and feelings, there is hope. I will describe that hope in the next chapter.

[1] King, Martin Luther Jr. *I Have a Dream: Writings and Speeches that Changed the World.* Ed. James M. Washington. (1992) San Francisco (Paraphrased. My personal interpretation.)

CHAPTER 12

A More Excellent Way

"...I will show you the most excellent way. If I speak in the tongues of men or of angels, but do not have love, I am only a resounding gong or a clanging cymbal. If I have the gift of prophecy and can fathom all mysteries and all knowledge, and if I have a faith that can move mountains, but do not have love, I am nothing. If I give all I possess to the poor and give over my body to hardship that I may boast, but do not have love, I gain nothing.

Love is patient, love is kind. It does not envy, it does not boast, it is not proud. It does not dishonor others, it is not self-seeking, it is not easily angered, it keeps no record of wrongs. Love does not delight in evil but rejoices with the truth. It always protects, always trusts, always hopes, always perseveres.

Love never fails. But where there are prophecies, they will cease; where there are tongues, they will be stilled; where there is knowledge, it will pass away. For we know in part and we prophesy in part, but when completeness comes, what is in part disappears. When I was a child, I talked like a child, I thought like a child, I reasoned like a child. When I became a man, I put the ways of childhood behind me. For now we see only a reflection as in a mirror; then we shall see face to face. Now I know in part; then I shall know fully, even as I am fully known.

> And now these three remain: faith,
> hope and love. **But the greatest of these
> is love."**
>
> 1 Corinthians 12:31b –13:13

Love is right. Love is always right. As we have seen, love seeks the best for the beloved. Love is not satisfied with anything less than the beloved's best. The pages of this book have shown that attempts to justify homosexual sexual activity do not carry their burden of proof. Homosexual sexual relationships are unnatural. They are immoral. They are harmful. Where do we go from here? We love.

For those who do not struggle with sexual attractions to people of their own gender, love those who do through their difficulty. For those who do have these attractions, love people by not harming them. It harms other people when you use them as a means to an end by engaging in homosexual sexual relationships.

You may be thinking, that is easy for him. He does not struggle with homosexual thoughts and feelings. He gets to have a wife and children, and raise a family. If you are thinking this, you are right, at least in part. I do not have the *same* struggles as any other particular human being, but I do have my struggles. I do have thoughts and feelings that tempt me to do all kinds of things that are unnatural, harmful, and morally wrong. I have to struggle to avoid doing evil and work hard to do what is good, just like you. I fail sometimes just like you.

Some may ask whether I think people with homosexual attractions ought to be celibate all of their lives. They may ask how I could want people to live alone and not have a family. How could I not want them to have someone with whom to share their lives? Why would I want someone to not be with the person who he is attracted to and who he loves?

I will do my best to answer these questions. As to celibacy, the answer is yes and no. We have seen that homosexual sex is morally wrong. Because of that fact, people ought not to engage in homosexual sex. However, the fact that one does not engage in homosexual sex does not mean the person must be celibate all of her life. Many people have overcome homosexual thoughts and feelings and married a person of the opposite sex. Please do not be deceived by those who claim that people with homosexual attractions cannot change. That is a lie. At least some people have overcome powerful homosexual thoughts and feelings and come out of the homosexual lifestyle, and entered into natural marriages.

Those who claim that people with homosexual attractions cannot change tell stories of people who have divorced their wives or husbands and re-entered the homosexual lifestyle, or entered the homosexual lifestyle for the first time, because they could not overcome their homosexual thoughts and feelings. These stories are not evidence of anything but selfishness. Many wives had boyfriends other than their husbands before they were married. But if they leave their husbands because they cannot overcome their thoughts and feelings for other men, they are being selfish. The fact that they are married to their husbands shows they *can* live in a marriage, whether they are attracted to other men or not. Being unhappy because you want to do something other than stay married and love your husband or wife is selfishness. Many men have strong thoughts and feelings that make them want to have sex with women other than their wives. If they do have sex with women other than their wives, we say they are acting immorally. We do not say that they are only being honest about who they are.

Of course, this may not apply to all people with homosexual thoughts and feelings. There may be some people who never develop an attraction to people of the opposite gender. For those who cannot bring themselves to be in a natural marriage, I do say that celibacy is what is morally right. Celibacy can be a noble calling. All of us were celibate for years before we had sex for the first time. We did not die because of celibacy; we were not even injured by celibacy. Many of us were not even lonely because of celibacy. Loneliness is difficult. It is difficult because we were designed to have a helpmate; someone with whom to share our lives. We were also clearly designed for that helpmate to be a person of the opposite sex. Male and female genitals were designed to complement one another; that fact could not be more obvious. So, if people are unable to enter into a sexual relationship with a helpmate and partner who they were obviously physically designed for, they ought not to enter into a sexual relationship with someone who they were not physically designed for simply because that is what they want in their thoughts and feelings.

The last question I posed was: Why would I not want someone to be with the person who they are attracted to and who they love? Let me use an illustration.

Jerry loves Jennifer. He is intensely attracted to Jennifer. Jennifer loves Jerry. Jennifer is intensely attracted to Jerry. They both want to be married and have children. Their thoughts and feelings desire only one another. Jennifer's and Jerry's family are opposed to their relationship. Because of this, both Jennifer and Jerry have tried hard to ignore their thoughts and feelings for one another. They have both tried to be attracted to other people. They have both failed. Try as they might, they cannot get rid of their feelings for one another. They want to marry and have sex and share life together. They want to be partners for life and live in a monogamous relationship and have children.

But I agree with their family. I think they should not marry one another. I believe that if they cannot find a way to marry someone other than each other, they should remain celibate. Why am I so heartless? Why would I not want them to be with the person who they are attracted to and who they love? Because, Jerry and Jennifer are brother and sister.

You may object. You may say 'Incest is not the same as homosexual sex.' I agree. Incest is not exactly the same thing as homosexual sex. But, the issue is the same. Jerry and Jennifer love each other in much the same way as any other person loves someone, the only real difference is that Jerry and Jennifer's love is obviously unnatural. You may object because, in this case, their children could be affected negatively because they are close relatives. Would it really make a difference if Jennifer was infertile? Of course not. Our objection to incest is not based only on the possibility of birth defects. Consider the fact that society allows women with Down's syndrome to marry. These women are substantially more likely to mother children who also have Down's syndrome than a sister and brother are to have children with birth defects. The fact is that incest is wrong. It is obviously wrong to all but those who wish to engage in incest themselves, and those who are morally corrupt. Consider the fact that among most people in the world today and throughout all of history, homosexual sex is, and has been, viewed the same way. It is obviously unnatural. Obviously morally wrong.

The point of this illustration is not to cause shame for people struggling with homosexual thoughts and feelings. The point is this: my conviction that it is morally right for some people to remain celibate if they cannot enter into natural marriage is not a heartless conviction. My *personal feelings* about celibacy have nothing to do with the truth about whether or not some people *ought* to remain celibate.

There is something more. I believe there is a real answer for people who suffer and struggle. That answer is found in redemption of the whole person; redemption of every part of who you *are.*

A long time ago, although not so very long ago, God created the universe. Then God created men and women. When He created us, He gave us a wonderful gift. He gave us the gift of choice. With this gift, we were able to love Him and to love one another. We were able to accomplish things. We could create paintings and music and drama and write books. We were also able to love and to be loved, and to enjoy loving and being loved. Unfortunately we used our gift of choice unwisely. We used it to defy and disobey God. We rebelled. We thought we would be happier if we simply chose to do what we wanted to do instead of living within the plan God had for us. When we made our unwise choice, sin came into the world. Great evil was done. Because of our wickedness, we became as we are now: hopeless, filled with thoughts and feelings that desire evil. If you have ever lied, or stolen, or gossiped, or treated someone poorly, you know what I write here is true. You have felt guilt. You have felt shame. There is a reason you feel guilty and ashamed. You feel this way because you know that what you have done is wrong. You know, if you are honest with yourself, that if there is a God who created this universe, you are His enemy. You have rebelled against Him. Because of that you cannot have a relationship with Him. You are doomed to receive the punishment you deserve, to be separated from God and from all of God's goodness.

But there is more to this story.

God still loves us; even though we are evil. Even though we normally spend much of our time devising ways to please ourselves and we do not give God our devotion, and we do not give Him our love, He still loves us.

Because He loves you so much, He did something extraordinary. He came to earth as a man in the person of His only begotten Son, Jesus Christ. This He did even though He knew He would be mistreated, abused, and murdered. All this He did because God loves you. When Jesus Christ gave Himself as a sacrifice on the cross, He took on all of your sins. Every dirty thought, every envious and selfish word and action you have ever done, or will do, was paid for through the death of Jesus Christ.

But that is not the end of the story.

Three days after the death of Jesus, He rose from the dead. When He rose, He defeated death, hell, and Satan.

Because of all of this you can live. You can be reborn into life and freedom. This freedom you can have was not free for Him. He paid your price. All you have to do is accept His gift of forgiveness. God wants to forgive you because God loves you. The Creator of this universe loves you. Gay and straight, gossips, slanderers, murderers, thieves and gluttons that we are, He loves us. He also told us that we will live beyond death. We will live either to see Him, or to be separated from Him in hell. Jesus Christ proclaimed Himself to be the one and only begotten Son of God. He claimed to be the only way to heaven, the only way to restore *your* relationship with God.

Take a minute right now. Put this book down and look out the window or go outside. If it is nighttime look at the stars. If it is daytime look at creation. Look at your hands and your feet. Think about your eyes that are doing all of this looking. The God who created these wonders loves you.

He tells us that "if you declare with your mouth, 'Jesus is Lord,' and believe in your heart that God raised him from the dead, you will be saved" (Romans 10:9).

You will be saved.

That is good news, if I have ever heard good news. It is because I have declared that Jesus Christ is Lord, He is my King, my Savior, my Ruler and my Friend, and it is because I believe God raised Jesus from the dead, that I also love you so much. I think you are amazing. You are God's amazing creation. It does not matter what you have done. It does matter what thoughts and feelings you struggle with; I love you. I wrote this book because I love you.

I want you to recognize the moral failure of homosexual sexual activity. But that is only the beginning. What I truly desire is that you would find True Love in the love Jesus Christ has for you. He loves you! He desires that you surrender to Him. He knows it is difficult. He knows you have suffered. He knows all your pains and He *will* comfort you. His burden is light[1] but you have to give up your burden first.

---

[1] "For my yoke is easy and my burden is light" (Matthew 11:30).

It is like a trust fall.[2] Staying up on your perch seems much safer than falling backward. You feel in control. But, when you give up your control and let go, you find that you are safe. The arms of others catch you. You can trust God. He will catch you in His arms; and when you are in *those* arms, nothing else will matter.

You must humble yourself enough to see that you have failed to do what is right; you have elevated your desires above your duties. You must realize that justice demands that you and I should be condemned. But He has paid the price. He struggled just like you and me, but He was victorious and He allowed Himself to be sacrificed for you. Will you, even now, turn from your sin and accept Him? He waits for you.

---

[2] A trust fall is a classic 'team building exercise' where one person is perched on some high point and the rest of the group stands be hind and below that person with their arms out. The person then falls backward and is safely caught by the group.

APPENDIX I

THE LEGAL ISSUE

Many readers have probably wondered what the state of the law is on the issue of homosexuality and how the law has developed. This appendix will give a short history of the law, how it has developed, and how it may develop in the future.

Past Law

In 1965, the United States Supreme Court ruled on a case called Griswold v. Connecticut.[1] The Court decided that the Constitution provides a 'right to privacy.' This new 'right to privacy' was used to create a Constitutional right to abortion in 1973, in the now famous Roe v. Wade[2] decision of the Court.

This 'right to privacy' was probably the 'crack in the door' of the law that has allowed the end of traditional

---

[1] *Griswold v. Connecticut*, 381 U.S. 479 (1965)

[2] *Roe v. Wade*, 410 U.S. 113 (1973)

sexual morality to creep in. In 1986, the Court decided another case, Bowers v. Hardwick.[3] In this case, an attempt was made to have the court find that bans against homosexual sodomy[4] were unconstitutional. Essentially, one side wanted the Court to find that no state could make homosexual sex a criminal offense. The Court did not agree, and upheld anti-sodomy laws as constitutional.

In his concurring opinion, Chief Justice Burger wrote:

> As the Court notes ... the proscriptions against sodomy have very "ancient roots." Decisions of individuals relating to homosexual conduct have been subject to state intervention throughout the history of Western civilization. Condemnation of those practices is firmly rooted in Judeo-Christian moral and ethical standards. Homosexual sodomy was a capital crime under Roman law...Blackstone described [sodomy as] "the infamous *crime against nature*" ... To hold that the act of

---

[3] *Bowers v. Hardwick*, 478 U.S. 186 (1986)

[4] Sodomy-Anal or oral sex

homosexual sodomy is somehow protected as a fundamental right would be to cast aside millennia of moral teaching.[5]

Justice White, who wrote the majority opinion, commented that, "In fact, until 1961, all 50 States outlawed sodomy."[6]

Fast forward to 2003, 17 years later, when the Court came out with a new opinion in a case titled Lawrence v. Texas.[7] In Lawrence v. Texas, the Court overruled the prior decision in Bowers v. Hardwick. This time the court did say that states could no longer outlaw sodomy.

In his dissenting opinion[8] Justice Antonin Scalia said:

Today's opinion is the product of a Court, which is the product of a law-profession culture, that has largely signed on to the so-

---

[5] *Bowers v. Hardwick*, 478 U.S. 186 (1986)

[6] *Bowers v. Hardwick*, 478 U.S. 186 (1986)

[7] *Lawrence v. Texas*, 539 U.S. 558 (2003)

[8] A dissenting opinion is an opinion written by a justice who does not agree with the decision made by the majority of the court.

called homosexual agenda, by which I mean the agenda promoted by some homosexual activists directed at eliminating the moral opprobrium[9] that has traditionally attached to homosexual conduct (my footnote).[10]

He went on to note: "What a massive disruption of the current social order, therefore, the overruling of *Bowers* entails."[11]

Justice Scalia also wrote:

...the Court has taken sides in the culture war, departing from its role of assuring, as neutral observer, that the democratic rules of engagement are observed. Many Americans do not want persons who openly engage in homosexual conduct as partners in their business, as scoutmasters for their children, as teachers in their children's schools, or as boarders in their home. They

[9] Opprobrium- Social criticism; shamefulness

[10] *Lawrence v. Texas,* 539 U.S. 558 (2003)

[11] *Lawrence v. Texas,* 539 U.S. 558 (2003)

view this as protecting themselves and their families from a lifestyle that they believe to be immoral and destructive.[12]

Justice Scalia discussed the fact that based on the Court's decision in this case; a constitutional right to homosexual "marriage" would follow. He wrote:

> State laws against bigamy, same-sex marriage, adult incest, prostitution, masturbation, adultery, fornication, bestiality, and obscenity are likewise sustainable only in light of *Bowers'* validation of laws based on moral choices. Every single one of these laws is called into question by today's decision.[13]

Most telling was Justice Scalia's observation that, "This effectively decrees the end of all morals legislation."[14] (Translation-The Supreme court is basically saying that laws, based on morals alone, will no longer be valid.)

---

[12] *Lawrence v. Texas*, 539 U.S. 558 (2003)

[13] *Lawrence v. Texas*, 539 U.S. 558 (2003)

[14] *Lawrence v. Texas*, 539 U.S. 558 (2003)

Think about Justice Scalia's last quote. He recognized that the United States Supreme Court was rejecting the idea that a law can be based on morality alone. In other words, because the Court, in Lawrence v. Texas,[15] found that homosexual sex could not be regulated as a crime, the Court will have to find that other laws based on morality alone cannot be enforced either.

Here is the problem: basically all laws are based in morality. That is right; in some manner, almost every law is based in morality. This is easy to see with laws against murder and kidnapping or laws against defrauding people. However, it may be harder to see how tax laws or traffic laws are based in morality.[16] As for tax laws, they are based upon the idea that the existence of the government itself is a moral good, and the fact that the government can only exist if the people who are governed pay the cost of the government. You can find this same theme with basically any law. Almost all laws will trace back to some moral good that is being sought or some moral evil that is being avoided.

---

[15] *Lawrence v. Texas*, 539 U.S. 558 (2003)

[16] As to traffic laws, see chapter 5 of this book for how these laws are related to morality.

The government exists to do what is good and to protect its citizens from evil. Please note that I am not suggesting that laws against sodomy are necessary or should be brought back. That is not the point. The point is, that by finding a 'right to privacy' for anything that goes on in a bedroom between consenting adults, the United States Supreme court basically decided that states were not allowed to criminalize certain conduct based on the fact that the state found the conduct to be morally wrong.

I do not think that avoiding criminal punishment is the main reason people were fighting against these types of laws. In Appendix II, I will go into the reason I believe people fought these types of laws in more detail.

We have now seen when and how the practice of homosexual sodomy was legalized in the United States of America. Now we will look at a timeline of Homosexual "marriage" laws.

Present Law

The first state to legally recognize homosexual "marriage" was Massachusetts. The Supreme Judicial

Court of Massachusetts decided that the Constitution of Massachusetts mandated that homosexuals have the same right to "marriage" as heterosexuals.[17] It is probably no surprise to the reader that Massachusetts decided that homosexual "marriage" should be legal on November 18, 2003, only 5 months after the United States Supreme Court decision in Lawrence v. Texas.[18] Then, in 2008, the highest courts in California[19] and Connecticut[20] legalized homosexual "marriage." In 2009, The Iowa Supreme Court held that homosexual "marriage" should be legal.[21] In the same year, legislatures in Vermont, Maine,[22] New Hampshire, and Washington D.C. passed laws allowing homosexual "marriage." In 2011, New York's legislature passed a bill making homosexual "marriage" legal. In 2012,

---

[17] *Goodridge v. Dept. of Public Health*, 798 N.E.2d 941 (Mass. 2003)

[18] *Lawrence v. Texas*, 539 U.S. 558 (2003)

[19] *In re Marriage Cases* (2008) 43 Cal.4th 757; The California Court's ruling was overruled by a vote of the citizens of California when they passed a Constitutional amendment against homosexual "marriages."

[20] **Kerrigan v. Commissioner of Public Health**, 289 Conn. 135, 957 A.2d 407 (2008)

[21] *Varnum v. Brien*, 763 N.W.2d 862 (Iowa 2009)

[22] Maine's law was repealed by a referendum vote of the people.

Maine, Maryland, and Washington State had referendum votes of the people to legalize homosexual "marriage." This was the first time that any state had legalized homosexual "marriage" by a vote of the people. Also, on May 9, 2012, Barack Obama became the first sitting President of the United States of America to openly support homosexual "marriage." So far, in 2013, Rhode Island, Delaware and Minnesota have all passed bills legalizing homosexual "marriage."

During the same time period, these states, and several others, approved laws recognizing some form of homosexual unions. Also, during the same time period, many states passed laws *against* homosexual "marriage." Currently, the constitutions of 31 states ban homosexual "marriage."

Now that I have outlined the recent history of laws on homosexual "marriage," I will give you my opinion about what new laws we may see in the future.

Future Laws

I see the direction of the law as beginning to infringe on religious and free speech rights. I think this will happen by the creation and spread of so-called 'hate speech' laws. I predict that some lawmakers will claim we need laws to protect people from the hateful speech of others. Such 'hate speech' will not be protected speech under the United States Constitution. In other words, the first amendment to the United States Constitution will not protect those who use 'hate speech.'

I expect any speech that suggests homosexuality is morally wrong will be labeled as 'hate speech.' If and when that happens, anyone who writes a book like this one, or any priest or pastor who declares that the Bible teaches that homosexuality is sinful, will be labeled a criminal.

Do you think this seems unlikely? If so, reflect on how unlikely the idea of homosexual "marriage" was 30 years ago.

What I have written in this Appendix is an outline of the legalization of homosexual sodomy, a timeline of homosexual "marriage" laws in the United States of America, and my forecast of what I think will happen with laws related to homosexuality in the future. To see why it matters and what I believe is really going on, see Appendix II.

APPENDIX II

Society's Progression and Why Words Matter

Society's Progression

In Appendix I, I said I thought there was a reason, other than avoiding criminal prosecution, that people advocated to get rid of state laws against sodomy. That reason is acceptance. These people do not just want to avoid the shame associated with criminal punishment; they want to avoid the shame associated with homosexual sex. This book has already discussed why that shame exists. It is the same kind of shame we feel when we do anything morally wrong. Unfortunately, as many people have begun to take less time to thoughtfully analyze their moral choices, the laws enacted by the government have become a strong influence on people's beliefs about what is morally right. In chapter five of this book, I wrote about moral arguing. Many of us have probably had one of those arguments that went something like this:

> **George:** "John. You shouldn't do that. It is wrong."
> **John:** "What do you mean George? I'm not doing anything illegal."

John is part of a group of people who, to some extent, have bought into the idea that if something is legal, it must not be morally wrong. I am not suggesting that all people, or even most people, believe this way. However, I do think many of us are too concerned with what is legal, rather than what is morally right. Not everything that is immoral is illegal.

I recognize that our laws are passed by a majority of the people and therefore laws often reflect the moral understanding of the people who vote for them. However, just because a group may be able to get a majority of people to vote to make a particular behavior legal does not mean the legalized behavior is morally right. If that was the case, homosexual "marriage" would have been morally wrong before some people voted to make it morally right. That does not make sense. Homosexual "marriage" is either morally right or it is morally wrong. We cannot change that fact, no matter how many of us vote for it or against it.

My point is that the advocates for 'homosexual rights' do not want to be left alone to do what they want to do. They want society to declare that their behavior is morally right and acceptable. They believe that, as sodomy is made legal, and homosexual "marriage" becomes common, people will start to lose their belief that homosexual sex is morally wrong. And they are probably right. The more common immorality becomes, the more people will start to lose their commitment to moral principles. If you are old enough, think about the way society looks at fornication and childbirth out of wedlock now, as compared to 40 years ago. Like the frog in boiling water,[1] we have become accustomed to 'the way things

---

[1] It is said that if a live frog is put into a pot of water, and the temperature is raised gradually enough, the frog will stay in the pot until it boils to death.

are.' If society accepts this behavior through law, eventually many people will no longer consider homosexual sex to be morally wrong.

We must see the legal strategy of 'homosexual rights' advocates in terms of a progression. First, we saw the removal of a negative law, a law *banning* a behavior was removed. States could no longer criminalize homosexual sex. Then we saw a move to create a positive law, a law *allowing* homosexual "marriage." One could choose to look at each law as negative and positive. In other words, the removal of the *ban* on sodomy could be viewed as a new *right* to engage in sodomy, and the new *right* to homosexual "marriage" could be viewed as the removal of a *ban* on homosexual "marriage." However, I believe the most reasonable way to view the removal of the ban on sodomy is to see it as a rule stating that the government cannot *ban* something just because they see it as morally wrong, but homosexual "marriage" is different. The creation of a new kind of "marriage" is an attempt to *celebrate* and *encourage* a particular type of union; to declare that these unions are morally right. The difference is between not being able to say no, and being forced to say yes. The government has traditionally encouraged marriage. To get the government to encourage this new form of "marriage" is to finally get society to remove the shame associated with homosexual sex. As I suggested in Appendix I, I think the next step, after this forced acceptance of homosexual "marriage," will be criminal punishment of those who disagree. If this happens, we will no longer be able to debate the morality of homosexual sex, and people like me, who desire to do nothing more than love through truth, may be in prison.

Why Words Matter

You may have noticed that every time I write the words homosexual "marriage," I put the word "marriage" in quotes. I do this for a very good reason. When I was in law school I was fond of using the phrase "words mean stuff." Words do mean stuff. If they did not mean anything, I could not write this book and you could not read it. The definitions of words are important. We cannot communicate well if we both have different definitions of the same words. When I use the word marriage, I mean the union between a man and a woman for life. That is what marriage is. That is what marriage has always been. The words homosexual "marriage" are nonsense to anyone who understands what the word marriage means.

Some may argue that at one time, and still in some places, polygamy is a type of marriage. It is true that there have been some people, and there still are people who see polygamy as a type of marriage. I do not believe that polygamous marriages are morally right. But, I will tell you why using polygamy to mean marriage is not the same kind of mistake as using the term homosexual "marriage." Polygamy is just multiple marriages. In other words, a polygamist is a person who has entered into multiple independent marriages. For the polygamist, each marriage is the union of one man and one woman for life. That is entirely different than using the word "marriage" to mean the union of one man and another man, or one woman and another woman. Some things just have meanings that cannot be changed. People have tried to say 'isn't the important thing about marriage that it is a loving relationship between two people? Why should the gender of the people involved matter?' I agree with these people that marriage is, ideally, a loving relationship between two people. However, words mean stuff. We cannot always try to derive the 'important aspects' of something and then call anything with those aspects by the same name. First of all, we will not all agree on what the important aspects of something are. I think the genders of the people involved in a marriage are important. For one thing, the bodies of a man and a woman can be naturally married to one another sexually. As we have seen, this is not true for homosexuals. Consider the following conversation between George and John:

George: "John, I think we should call dogs cats."

John: "Why on earth would we do that?"

George: "Aren't the important things about cats that they are furry and nice to pet and that they are good companions for humans?"

John: "I suppose that is why most people like them."

George: "Aren't all those things true for dogs as well?"

John: "I guess so."

George: "There you have it. Obviously dogs are cats."

This silly conversation is used only to show that words are important. We cannot simply redefine words that have had important meanings for millennia just because a particular group feels left out of the definition. But that is what our society is being asked to do. You are being asked to redefine traditional marriage, and to redefine morality.[2] I, for one, am not inclined to do so for two reasons. The first reason is that I like marriage. I think marriage is important and special. The second is that I cannot redefine marriage. I cannot redefine it because I did not invent it. Marriage has existed for thousands of years. It was not invented by the government, and therefore the government cannot choose to redefine it. We can choose to call a union between two people of the same gender "marriage" if we want to, but that will not redefine the word; it will only show our ignorance of the meaning of the word.

Marriage is not the only word that has this problem. In May of 2013, the Boy Scouts of America changed their policy to allow boys who are openly homosexual to join their group. Of course, sexual activity of any kind,

---

[2] For some far better writing on why the meanings of words are i mportant *see*: Lewis, C.S.; *The Complete C.S. Lewis Signature Class ics.* (2002), New York; p. 9–10

heterosexual or homosexual, is prohibited for any Boy Scout (at any time) because it is considered to be immoral. So it would seem like the Boy Scouts are just being inclusive, tolerant, and kind to allow these homosexual boys into their ranks. After all, they are not engaging in homosexual sex and that is all I have objected to in this book.

Here is the problem. It is true that I have only shown that homosexual *sex* is wrong in this book. It is the act of engaging in homosexual sex that is wrong, not the feelings and desires of a person to engage in homosexual sex. So why do I have a problem with the Boy Scouts? I have a problem because it is meaningless to *identify* oneself as a homosexual unless one engages in homosexual sex, or intends to do so in the future. Society has identified people with attractions to people of their own gender as homosexuals. This definition makes no sense. We do not call people who are attracted to horseback riding horseback riders. We call people who actually ride horses horseback riders. It would be silly to do otherwise. We use words like 'sexual orientation' and homosexuality to refer to people who have particular desires, but we do not do that with other words.

> **John:** "George, I want you to know that earlier today when you caught me stealing your weed-eater I really wanted to lie to you and tell you that I was not stealing it.
>
> **George:** "Well John, you are certainly a thief, but at least you are not a liar."

Do you see why George called John a thief but not a liar? Because John did not lie, he only *wanted* to lie. By using the same word to describe someone who has a desire to do something with the word we use for people who actually do that thing, we are forcing an unfair and incorrect *identity* on people. When we define individuals by their thoughts and feelings instead of defining them by their behavior, especially when the thoughts and feelings, in themselves, are not wrong, but the behavior *is* morally wrong, we have a big problem.

Of course boys with sexual attractions to people of their own gender should be allowed into the Boy Scouts. That is right. I think that boys who are sexually attracted to other boys should be allowed in the Boy Scouts. Here is the difference. I do not think boys who intend to engage in homosexual sex (now or later) should be allowed in the Boy Scouts. The official statement from the Boy Scouts of America says that they will "remove the restriction denying membership to youth on the basis of sexual orientation alone."[3] If 'sexual orientation' simply means one is attracted to people of his own gender, without any intent to act on those desires, now or later, then this statement would be fine. The problem is almost no one defines the words 'sexual orientation' that way. People define 'sexual orientation' as an identity. They define it as the desire to have sex with people of one's own gender and, they assume, the intent to live a life that includes acting out on that desire. Homosexual attraction and 'sexual orientation' do not mean the same thing. Words mean stuff.

---

[3] Retrieved from: http://www.scouting.org/licensing/sitecore /content/membershipstandards/resolution/faq.aspx. Last visited June 17, 2013.

APPENDIX III
Resources

I have provided the names and web addresses of several resources below for those who desire help in their struggle with homosexual attractions. I cannot personally endorse any particular group because I am not familiar enough with any of them to do so. I recommend that you read the information on their websites and contact them directly for more information.

• Homosexuals Anonymous:
http://www.ha-fs.org/

• Exodus International:
http://exodusinternational.org/

- Courage: A Roman Catholic Apostolate:
http://couragerc.net/

- Restoring Hope:
http://www.restoringhope.net/

- Pure Intimacy:
http://www.pureintimacy.org/homosexuality/

- There are also groups and counselors available at many local churches. Search for a Bible based, solid church in your area through the web or through word of mouth.

20079927R00123

Made in the USA
Charleston, SC
26 June 2013